The Sherlock Holmes Quiz Book

" . . . he stands before us as a symbol — a symbol, if you please, of all that we are not, but ever would be. His figure is sufficiently remote to make our secret aspirations for transference seem unshameful, yet close enough to give them plausibility. We see him as the fine expression of our urge to trample evil and to set aright the wrongs with which the world is plagued. He is Galahad and Socrates, bringing high adventure to our dull existences and calm, judicial logic to our biased minds. He is the success of all our failures; the bold escape from our imprisonment."

— Edgar Smith

The Sherlock Holmes Quiz Book

ALBERT J. MENENDEZ

DRAKE PUBLISHERS INC
New York — London

Published in 1978 by
Drake Publishers, Inc.
801 Second Avenue
New York, N.Y. 10017

Library of Congress Cataloging in Publication Data

Menendez, Albert J.
  The Sherlock Holmes quiz book.

  1. Doyle, Sir Arthur Conan, 1859-1930. I. Title.
PR4623.M4   823'.9'12   74-13640
ISBN 0-87749-732-X

Printed in the United States of America.

1 2 3 4 5 6 7 8 9 0

DEDICATED TO SHIRLEY, MY WIFE

Line drawings appearing throughout this book are reproductions of etchings by Sidney Paget that originally appeared in the Strand *magazine between 1890 and 1910.*

Table of Contents

Introduction   vii

List of Quizzes

Introduction

A Sherlock Holmes quiz book, you say? What could one possibly want with such a specialized and eccentric little book? Well, the best rejoinder I can think of is that thousands, if not millions, of individuals throughout this planet cherish the memory of the greatest consulting detective who ever lived — the master who is the subject of this trifling exercise in diversion.

I hope there will be something for everyone in the mélange that follows the inevitable introduction. It is designed to stimulate, to challenge, and to awaken the latent scholarly instincts of would-be Sherlockians everywhere. It should also be a lot of pure, unadulterated fun.

I suppose this is as good a place as any for me to hark back to the dim recesses of my past and share my own discovery of Sherlock Holmes. Every Sherlockian enthusiast could undoubtedly share similar stories of the joy of discovering these gems. My case is probably unremarkable. I first read *The Hound of the Baskervilles* when in my mid-teens and it afforded me a singular pleasure. Perhaps it was the atmosphere of the moors, the timing and setting, or the superbly constructed and chilling plot — or a combination of all of these — but after reading *The Hound*, I knew I was hooked for life. I plunged into the canon with abandon and read it for pure enjoyment. I never dreamed that the world of Sherlockian commentary and scholarship even existed.

I felt a warm sense of appreciation for both Holmes and Watson and felt as if I really knew these admirable gentlemen. They were and remain my dearest friends. Would that I could take a hansom cab to No. 221B and ascend those seventeen steps on a cold and wintry evening! Perhaps it was my innate love of mysteries and complexities, my admiration for reason, or my blossoming love affair with England (I'm an inveterate Anglophile for whom there will always be an England). Perhaps it was even a nostalgic yearning for simpler times and values. Anyway, I bravely decided to write my first major college paper on Sherlock Holmes. I think the title was something ponderous like "The Sherlock Holmes Saga and its Epic Influence." As I look back now from the vantage point of 1974, it was a horrid paper, terribly pompous and pseudoserious. It was an attempted analysis of Sherlock Holmes's influence on mystery fiction, but I now realize I only scratched the surface. However, I did get my first taste of Sherlockian scholarship, commentary, and pastiches, and shortly thereafter I read Baring-Gould's *Sherlock Holmes of Baker Street: The Life of the World's First Consulting Detective* and Mollie and Michael Hardwick's *Sherlock Holmes Companion*.

But then I committed an unpardonable sin — apostasy. I fell from grace and failed to keep up my Sherlockian pursuits. Only occasionally did I read again those familiar tales from the canon. Fortunately, my redemption drew nigh. A true Sherlockian always returns to the fold. In early 1972 I discovered Vincent Starrett's *Private Life of Sherlock Holmes* and tumbled back on the path of righteousness. I was living in Atlanta at that time and heard a rumor via the rare booksellers' underground that a Sherlockian scion society, appropriately named The Confederates of Wisteria Lodge, existed in Atlanta and had actually celebrated Sherlock's birthday on January 6 in Underground Atlanta. I promptly found my way to the group's next meeting, where I knew I was among simpatico people. A delightful quiz accompanied a pleasant gathering and a sumptuous feast.

As fate would have it, only a few days later I accepted a job in Washington, D.C., packed up, and headed north. I was told that a really lively scion society, with the slightly sinister name of The Red Circle and under the aegis of one Peter Blau, existed in the Federal City. In due time I contacted Herr Blau and his compatriots and found a fascinating and delightful band of Irregulars. It was about this time that I discovered some of those marvelous books published by Drake Publishers Inc. (Michael Harrison's *The London of Sherlock Holmes* and *In the Footsteps of Sherlock Holmes*, and Martin Dakin's *A Sherlock Homes Commentary*).

I've been a quiz book enthusiast for as long as I can remember. Quizzes are endlessly fascinating and challenging to me. They awaken my interests and stimulate my investigatory instincts and frequently deflate my ego. How little we really know about this world and its myriad components! Anyway, this book, a first in the field of Sherlockiana, contains over 1,000 questions of Sherlockian information. Most come directly from the canon. A few are based on bits and pieces of Sherlockian lore. Most of the quizzes are grouped by similar subject area since I have a rather methodical mind that loves to classify and categorize everything. I do have three quizzes which are farragoes of information — a mixed bag of anything and everything that should delight even the most casual reader of the canon.

My hope is that each of you will enjoy this little book and that it will serve as a springboard for your own personal investigations of the byways of Baker Street. Don't let an initial low score get you down. It only means that you need to plunge in and start reading or rereading the sacred writings with more attention to detail. Perhaps this modest effort will help to awaken or reawaken interest in those wonderful days not so very long ago.

Someone once asked me (rather unkindly I thought) why I devoted so much valuable time to a man who never lived. Sherlock Holmes and Dr. Watson never lived, they say? Rubbish! Sherlock Holmes and Dr. Watson are as much a part of the hallowed legacy of England as Shakespeare, Milton, or Churchill. As enduring a part of the landscape of that sceptered isle as Stonehenge, Westminster Abbey or Canterbury Cathedral. And they will live in the hearts of those who love them for as long as man endures. For a few joyful hours, then, let us join Sherlock Holmes and Dr. Watson as they set out from Baker Street once again.

Albert J. Menendez
Silver Spring, Maryland

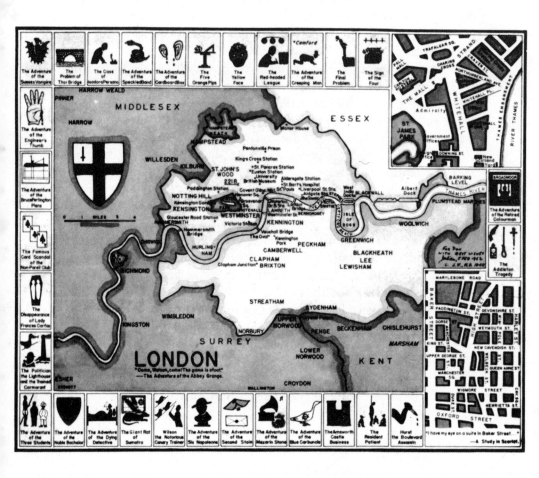

QUESTIONS

Who's Who I

(Answers To This Quiz Found On Pages 81-82)

Name the case in which each of these unforgettable characters appears:

1.	Mr. Acton	18.	Breckinridge
2.	Ronald Adair	19.	Josiah Brown
3.	Josiah Amberley	20.	Silas Brown
4.	Ames	21.	James Browner
5.	Hosmer Angel	22.	Richard Brunton
6.	Dr. Leslie Armstrong	23.	Patrick Cairns
7.	Henry Baker	24.	Capt. Peter Carey
8.	Ted Baldwin	25.	Robert Carruthers
9.	Bannister	26.	Cartwright
10.	James Barclay	27.	Arthur Charpentier
11.	Cecil James Barker	28.	Professor Coram
12.	Baynes	29.	Capt. Jack Croker
13.	Beddington	30.	Cunningham
14.	Trevor Bennett	31.	Colonel Sir James Damery
15.	Beppo	32.	Steve Dixie
16.	Blessington	33.	James M. Dodd
17.	Hugh Boone	34.	John Douglas

35.	Enoch J. Drebber	43.	Aloysius Garcia
36.	John Scott Eccles	44.	J. Neil Gibson
37.	Rev. J. C. Elman	45.	Gilchrist
38.	Colonel Emsworth	46.	Giuseppe Gorgiano
39.	Alec Fairbairn	47.	Philip Green
40.	Robert Ferguson	48.	Horace Harker
41.	John Ferrier	49.	Joseph Harrison
42.	Frankland	50.	Victor Hatherley

Who's Who II

(Answers To This Quiz Found On Pages 82-83)

51.	Reuben Hayes	60.	Sidney Johnson
52.	Colonel Hayter	61.	Peter Jones
53.	Arthur Holder	62.	William Kirwan
54.	Trelawney Hope	63.	Paul Kratides
55.	Jefferson Hope	64.	Harold Latimer
56.	Hudson	65.	Leverton
57.	Morse Hudson	66.	Eduardo Lucas
58.	Dr. Thorneycroft Huxtable	67.	Emilia Lucca
59.	Shinwell Johnson	68.	Charles McCarthy

69. John Hector McFarlane

70. John McGinty

71. Miles McLaren

72. Fitzroy McPherson

73. Teddy Marvin

74. John Mason

75. White Mason

76. Melas

77. Sam Merton

78. Brother Morris

79. James Mortimer

80. Francis Hay Moulton

81. Grant Munro

82. Ian Murdoch

83. John Hopley Neligan

84. Hugo Oberstein

85. Jonas Oldacre

86. John Openshaw

87. Cyril Overton

88. Peterson

89. Percy Phelps

90. Jack Prendergast

91. Professor Presbury

92. Hall Pycroft

93. John Rance

94. Daulat Ras

95. Duncan Ross

96. Rev. Roundhay

97. Dr. Grimesby Roylott

98. Jephro Rucastle

99. James Ryder

100. Neville St. Clair

Who's Who III

(Answers To This Quiz Found On Pages 83-84)

101. Mr. Sandeford

102. Selden

103. Dr. Shlessinger

104. Bartholomew Sholto

105. Fitzroy Simpson

106. Abe Slaney

107. Jonathan Small

108. Culverton Smith

109. Mordecai Smith

110. Willoughby Smith

111. Hilton Soames

112. Harold Stackhurst

113. Joseph Stangerson

114. John Stapleton

115. Colonel Lysander Stark

116. Godfrey Staunton

117. Peter Steiler

118. Dr. Leon Sterndale

119. Barney Stockdale

120. John Straker

121. Tonga

122. Dr. Percy Trevelyan

123. Victor Trevor

124. John Turner

125. Von Bork

126. Colonel Valentine Walter

127. Arthur Cadogan West

128. Isa Whitney

129. James Wilder

130. Williamson

131. Jabez Wilson

132. James Windibank

133. Windigate

134. Henry Wood

135. John Woodley

Which Case?

(Answers To This Quiz Found On Pages 85-86)

Can you name the case to which the following clues allude?

1. Though the precise chronology of Holmes's cases has occasioned a never-ending dispute among Sherlockians, this is considered to have been the first by all scholars.

2. This is definitely the last case.

3-4. These two cases were narrated by Holmes himself.

5. Holmes is the witness at a wedding.

6. References are made to the Ku Klux Klan.

7. The first *published* case.

8. The last *published* case.

9. The message "put the papers on the sundial" appears.

10. Holmes spends a morning in the British Museum Reading Room looking up the history of voodooism.

11-12. In these two cases Holmes saves an innocent person from a deliberately planned false murder charge.

13. A valuable manuscript is stolen.

14. In this case dealing with abduction, the abductors escape.

15. The crime is forgery.

16. Leprosy appears.

17-20. Name the four cases in which Holmes allowed the murderer to go free.

21-22. Name the two cases in which the murderers escape but are presumably drowned at sea.

23. The murderess escapes and is never heard from again.

24-25. Name the two cases involving theft of gems in which the thief was caught and jailed.

26-27. Name the two cases involving jewel theft in which the thief escaped.

28. In this case involving theft of classified documents the thief was not imprisoned for reasons of secrecy.

29. "Come Watson, come, the game is afoot."

30. At the conclusion of this case Holmes and Watson go to the opera.

31. In which case does Holmes say "Elementary, my dear Watson"?

32. Holmes straightens out a steel poker.

33-35. In these three later cases Holmes makes use of that new invention — the telephone.

36. Mrs. Hudson helps Holmes at considerable personal risk.

37. The Mormons appear prominently.

38. Holmes offers Watson a snuff box.

39. Watson calls this case "the supreme moment of my friend's career".

40. This case is written in third person and takes place entirely in the sitting room at 221B.

41. Holmes adorns the wall with a patriotic V.R. in bullet marks.

42. This case reveals Watson's love of racing and gambling.

43. Watson's checkbook is in Holmes' care.

44. A man with the extraordinary name Hynes Hynes appears.

45-46. In these two cases Holmes drives himself so hard that he collapses.

47. A non-existent German ocean is referred to.

48. A defrocked parson was supposed to perform a wedding ceremony.

49. Reference is made to Holmes' "small but very efficient organization".

50. Holmes says ". . . it is the season of forgiveness".

Name the Character
(Answers To This Quiz Found On Pages 87-88)

Can you identify these famous characters from the clues given? (direct quotes from the canon)

1. The daintiest thing under a bonnet on this planet.

2. A quaint, gnarled, dried-up person.

3. I have not seen a man who, if he turned his talents that way, was more calculated to fill the gap left by the illustrious Moriarty.

4. A touch of red in nose and cheeks, with a slight tremor of his extended hand.

5. He was a dashing, jovial old soldier in his usual mood, but there were occasions on which he seemed to show himself capable of considerable violence and vindictiveness.

6. He is my hated rival upon the Surrey shore . . . . He has several good cases to his credit.

7. He was a tall, handsome youth about thirty, well dressed and elegant, but with something in his bearing which suggested the shyness of the student rather than the self-possession of the man of the world.

8. An alert, sharp-featured simian man with thick eyebrows, and a very peculiar projection of the lower part of the face like the muzzle of a baboon.

9. A shock of orange hair, a pale face disfigured by a horrible scar, which by its contraction, has turned up the outer edge of his upper lip, a bull-dog chin, and a pair of very penetrating dark eyes.

10. He would always take drink when he was ashore, and a little drink would send him stark, staring mad.

11. She is what we call in England a tomboy, with a strong nature, wild and free, unfettered by any sort of traditions.

12. His life history was written in his heavy features and pompous manner. From his spats to his gold-rimmed spectacles he was a Conservative, a Churchman, a good citizen, orthodox and conventional to the last degree.

13. A big, solemn, rather pompous clergyman.

14. A red-veined nose jutted out like a vulture's beak, and two fierce grey eyes glared at me from under tufted brows.

15. From the great inland sea to the distant Wahsatch Mountains there was no name better known than that of _____.

16.   An Abraham Lincoln keyed to base uses instead of high ones would give some idea of the man.

17.   A tall fair man with lion-like hair and beard, and curiously penetrating light blue eyes . . . a man who was rapidly making his name in the English detective service.

18.   The fellow is . . . extraordinarily handsome, with a most fascinating manner, a gentle voice, and that air of romance and mystery which means so much to a woman. He is said to have the whole sex at his mercy and to have made ample use of the fact.

19.   She was a striking-looking woman, a little short and thick for symmetry, but with a beautiful olive complexion, large, dark Italian eyes, and a wealth of deep black hair.

20.   Alias of Don Juan Murillo. "The most lewd and bloodthirsty tyrant that had ever governed any country with a pretence to civilisation."

21.   He was a small, stout man with a red face and a peppery manner.

22.   She was plainly but neatly dressed, with a bright, quick face, freckled like a plover's egg, and with the brisk manner of a woman who has had her own way to make in the world.

23.   He was red-faced, burly, and plethoric, with a pair of very small, twinkling eyes, which looked keenly out from between swollen and puffy pouches.

24.   The richest as well as the most lovely widow upon earth.

25.   He is a brilliant fellow when he chooses to work—one of the brightest intellects of the University: but he is wayward, dissipated, and unprincipled.

26. A tall, clean-shaven man with the firm, austere expression which is only seen upon those who have to control horses or boys.

27. He earns his living partly as interpreter in the law courts, partly by acting as guide to any wealthy Orientals who may use the Northumberland Avenue hotels.

28. One could not look upon his cruel blue eyes, with their drooping, cynical lids, or upon the fierce, aggressive nose and the threatening, deep-lined brow, without reading Nature's plainest danger-signals.

29. He is extremely tall and thin, his forehead domes out in a white curve, and his two eyes are deeply sunken in his head. He is clean-shaven, pale, and ascetic-looking, retaining something of the professor in his features. His shoulders are rounded from much study, and his face protrudes forward, and is forever slowly oscillating from side to side in a curiously reptilian fashion.

30. I never looked at his pale, keen face . . . without associating him with grey archways and mullioned windows and all the venerable wreckage of a feudal keep.

31. A portly, large-featured man, grave, tall, and frock-coated, with the dignity of bearing which a lecturer needs.

32. A bright, handsome girl of a conventional English type.

33. A smart young City man, of the class who have been labelled Cockneys.

34. A quiet, inscrutable fellow . . . well up in his work, though his Greek is his weak subject.

35. A middle-aged man, portly and affable, with a considerable fund of local lore.

36. She was of the Swedish type, blonde and fair-haired, with the piquant contrast of a pair of beautiful dark eyes.

37. One of the most unscrupulous rascals that Australia has ever evolved—and for a young country it has turned out some very finished types.

38. He was a tall, handsome, swarthy fellow . . . with a panama hat, a bristling black beard, and a great aggressive hooked nose.

39. A decent, quiet, hard-working fellow, with no weak spot in him at all. And yet this is the lad who has met his death this morning in the professor's study under circumstances which can point only to murder.

40. A man rather over the middle size but of an exceeding thinness. I do not think that I have ever seen so thin a man.

41. I have lived so long among savages and beyond the law that I have got into the way of being a law unto myself.

42. A large woman with a heavy fur boa around her neck, and a large curling red feather in a broad-brimmed hat which was tilted in a coquettish Duchess-of-Devonshire fashion over her ear.

43. Her dark, clear-cut face was handsome, even in death.

44. Formerly James Armitage. He was a man of little culture, but with a considerable amount of rude strength both physically and mentally.

45. He was the only friend I made during the two years that I was at college . . . and that only through the accident of his bull-terrier freezing on to my ankle one morning as I went down to chapel.

46. The most astute secret service man in Europe.

47. There was nothing remarkable about the man save his bla
ing red head.

48. The ruddy, white-aproned landlord.

49. A slim, flame-like young woman with a pale, intense face,
youthful, and yet so worn with sin and sorrow that one read
the terrible years which left their leprous mark upon her.

50. The kind of maid you don't pick up nowadays.

Scene of Action I

(Answers To This Quiz Found On Pages 89-90)

1. Watson moved to his own quarters in which street (in *The Illustrious Client*)?

2. Who lived in Briony Lodge?

3. In which London hotel was Sir Henry Baskerville staying when one of his boots mysteriously vanished?

4. Who lived at Deep Dene House in Lower Norwood?

5. Who lived in Campden Mansions, Notting Hill?

6. In one of the unrecorded cases, Holmes went to which Russian city to investigate the Trepoff murder?

7. Who lived at Fairbank?

Match homes with occupants:

8.	Birlstone Manor House	A.	Neville St. Clair
9.	Briarbrae	B.	Professor Coram
10.	Charlington Hall	C.	John Douglas
11.	Cheeseman's	D.	Josiah Brown
12.	The Cedars, Lee	E.	Colonel Emsworth
13.	Hurlstone Manor House	F.	Percy Phelps
14.	Laburnum Lodge	G.	Robert Ferguson
15.	Lachine	H.	Mr. Williamson
16.	Tuxbury Old Park	I.	Reginald Musgrave
17.	Yoxley Old Place	J.	Colonel Barclay

18. Who lived at Pondicherry Lodge?

19. Who lived at Vernon Lodge?

20. Who lived at Merripit House?

21. Who lived in the St. Johns' Wood section of London?

22. In which case do Holmes and Watson visit the Russian Embassy in London?

23. In which case does the Saffron Hill area appear?

24. Langdale Pike spent most of his time in a club on which street?

25. Marie Devine lived at No. 11 on which street in Montpellier?

26. Mr. Cubitt stayed at a boarding house in which London street?

27. Mrs. Porter's family lived here.

28. Where did Aloysius Doran live?

29. Where in Norfolk did the Trevors live?

Name the church associated with these weddings:

30. Mary Sutherland and Hosmer Angel.

31. Lord Robert St. Simon and Hatty Doran.

32. Irene Adler and Godfrey Norton.

33. Curzon Square and Edmonston Street figure in which case?

34. Where was Tonga from?

35. Who lived at Albemarle Mansion?

36. Who lived at 13 Caulfield Gardens?

37. From which station did Holmes and Watson leave to go to Cambridge in *The Missing Three-Quarter*?

38. Where did Miss Edith Woodley live?

39. Which street did clerks at the Foreign Office use as a short cut?

40. From which station did Holmes and Watson leave, en route to Kent in *Abbey Grange*?

41. Who lived at Lafter Hall?

42. In which hotel did Philip Green and the King of Bohemia stay?

43. Who lived at No. 3 Mayfield Place, Peckham?

44. Of what club was Mycroft Holmes a member?

45. Near which cafe was a murderous attack made on Holmes?

46. After *Black Peter* was settled where did Holmes and Watson go?

47. Where, at one time, was Elias Openshaw a planter?

48. In the *Priory School* the Duchess of Holdernesse took residence in the south of which country?

49. Who lived at 136 Little Ryder Street?

50. Who lodged at 226 Gordon Square?

Scene of Action II

(Answers To This Quiz Found On Pages 90-91)

51. Where did Peterson buy a used hat and a Christmas goose?

52. In which village did Holmes and Watson lunch en route to Boscombe Valley?

53. Who lived on Great Orme Street?

54. Who lived in Grosvenor Square?

55. Who lived at Hales Lodge?

56. Who supposedly lived at No. 369 Half Moon Street?

57. Where did Colonel Spence Munro move?

58. Who lived at No. 17 Potter's Terrace?

59. Where did two men dump Mr. Warren?

60. Who lived at The Dingle, near Oxshott?

61. Who lived at 131 Pitt Street?

62. From which station did Watson catch his train for London from Lewisham?

63. Who lived at No. 3 Pinchin Lane, Lambeth?

64. Where was Irene Adler born?

65. Where did Trevor, Senior make his money in gold fields?

66. Name the Berkshire village where the Ronder circus carava stopped for the night en route to Wimbledon.

67. Where was Mary Fraser brought up?

68. Where had Count Sylvius once shot lions?

69. The Blue Carbuncle was found in which river?

70. From where did Trelawney Hope receive a memorandum?

71. Where did J. Neil Gibson look for gold?

72. Abe Slaney was "the most dangerous crook" in what city?

73. Where was Enoch J. Drebber from?

74. Where did Mr. Hebron and his child die of yellow fever?

75. To what city does this refer: " . . . that great cesspool into which all the loungers and idlers of the Empire are irresistibly drained."

Most of the cases occur in London or nearby counties. Match the case on the left with the county in which most of the action occurs:

76. The Dancing Men   A. Bedfordshire

77. The Lion's Mane   B. Berkshire

78. The Five Orange Pips   C. Cambridgeshire

79. The Cardboard Box   D. Cornwall

80. The Copper Beeches   E. Devonshire

81. The Blanched Soldier   F. East Anglia

82. The Engineer's Thumb   G. Hampshire

83. The Devil's Foot   H. Herefordshire

84. The Hound of the Baskervilles   I.   Kent

85. The Missing Three-Quarter   J.   Norfolk

86. The Reigate Squires   K.   Surrey

87. The Boscombe Valley Mystery   L.   Sussex

88. Wisteria Lodge

89. Gloria Scott

90. Abbey Grange

91. The Golden Pince-nez

92. Shoscombe Old Place

93. Silver Blaze

94. Thor Bridge

95. Solitary Cyclist

96. The Speckled Band

97. The Musgrave Ritual

98. Black Peter

99. Who lived at No. 427 Park Lane?

100. Where was Young Perkins killed?

Scene of Action III

(Answers To This Quiz Found On Pages 91-92)

101. Where did Holmes and Watson first meet?

102. Who lived at Torrington Lodge?

103. What was the name of the opium den in *The Man with the Twisted Lip*?

104. In which county was St. Oliver's private school located?

105. The Alpha Inn was near which famous landmark?

106. In which card club did Ronald Adair play his last game?

107. Where did Admiral Sinclair live?

108. Who lived at No. 104 Berkeley Square?

109. On what street did Holmes first live in London?

110. Where did Jabez Wilson have a pawn shop?

111. Who lived on Conduit Street?

112. Where was the home of the Armitages in *The Speckled Band*?

113. Near which town was Mrs. Roylott killed in a railway accident?

114. Where did Grant Munro take an hour's walk?

115. Who resided at No. 13 Firbank Villas?

116. In which county is Little Pearlington located?

117. Halliday's Private Hotel is near which railway station?

118. Who lived at Forton Old Hall?

119. Where did Mr. Fowler and Alice Rucastle go after they eloped?

120. Who lived at No. 13 Great George Street?

121. In what Devonshire village did James Mortimer live?

122. Where did the Guild of St. George meet?

123. Who lived at High Gable?

124. What was the second largest private banking firm in the City of London?

125. Where did Baron Gruner play polo?

126. Where did Godfrey Norton practice law?

127. In which Oxford Street shop did Watson buy boots?

128. Who was murdered at No. 3 Lauriston Gardens?

129. Who lived at Potham House?

130. Where did Holmes bank?

131. Where did Straubenzee have his gunsmith shop?

132. Who lived at No. 136 Moorside Gardens?

133. Where did Watson take his prescribed course for army surgeons?

134. Where did the Grant Munros have a villa?

135. Where did Colonel Sebastian Moran attend university?

136. From where did Isadore Klein's family come?

137. Holmes and Watson stayed in a cottage overlooking which body of water in *The Devil's Foot*?

138. Who had an office at No. 7 Pope's Court?

139. Where did Major Freebody live?

140. Where in England did Watson land when he returned from India?

141. Where was Douglas Maberley attache at the time of his death?

142. Who lived on Rue Austerlitz in Paris?

143. Where did Mrs. Porter's family live?

144. At which hall in London did the violinist Sarasate play?

145. Where did Lady Frances Carfax bank?

146. Whose Hampshire estate bordered on the residence of Jephro Rucastle?

147. To which county did Holmes retire to keep bees?

148. Who lived at Beauchamp Arriance, Cornwall?

149. What did Watson call the most primitive village in England?

150. What was Broadmoor?

Matching Sets

(Answers To This Quiz Found On Page 93)

The fifty-six short stories were originally published in five sets or collections: (a) The Adventures of Sherlock Holmes, (b) The Memoirs of Sherlock Holmes, (c) The Return of Sherlock Holmes, (d) His Last Bow, and (e) The Case Book of Sherlock Holmes. Can you match the story with its collection?

1. A Scandal in Bohemia

2. The "Gloria Scott"

3. The Empty House

4. Wisteria Lodge

5. The Sussex Vampire

6. The Norwood Builder

7. The Red Circle

8. The Lion's Mane

9. The Boscombe Valley Mystery

10. The Five Orange Pips

11. The Musgrave Ritual

12. The Naval Treaty

13. The Blue Carbuncle

14. The Final Problem

15. The Second Stain

16. The Devil's Foot

17. Thor Bridge

18. The Six Napoleons

19. The Beryl Coronet

20. The Retired Colourman

21. The Dying Detective

22. The Blanched Soldier

23. The Red-headed League

24. Silver Blaze

25. The Copper Beeches

Holmes and His Disguises

(Answers To This Quiz Found On Page 93)

There are fourteen disguises mentioned in the canon. Match the disguise with the case in which Holmes employs it (you may use a case more than once):

Disguises	Cases
1. an aged master mariner	A. His Last Bow
2. a drunken groom	B. The Dying Detective
3. an old man	C. The Sign of Four
4. a common loafer	D. A Scandal in Bohemia
5. Holmes fakes an epileptic seizure	E. The Man with the Twisted Lip
6. an Italian priest	F. The Beryl Coronet
7. an elderly bookseller	G. The Reigate Squires
8. a rakish young workman	H. The Mazarin Stone
9. a French workman	I. The Empty House
10. an unemployed workman	J. The Final Problem
11. an old woman	K. Charles Augustus Milverton
12. a dying man	L. The Disappearance of Lady Frances Carfax
13. an Irish-American espionage agent	
14. an amiable nonconformist clergyman	

The Animal Kingdom

(Answers To This Quiz Found On Page 94)

There are several references in the canon to various canines. In which cases do the following appear?

1. Toby.

2. Carlo, a mastiff.

3. "the curious incident of the dog in the night-time."

4. Pompey.

5. James Mortimer's curly-haired spaniel.

6. Carlo, a paralyzed spaniel.

7. Roy.

8. Fitzroy McPherson's little dog died "at the very place" he did.

9. Lady Falder's black spaniel.

10. Victor Trevor's bull terrier.

11. *Cyanea Capilata* appears in which case?

12. What was the name of the lion blamed for Ronder's murder in *The Veiled Lodger*?

13. What was the killer in *The Lion's Mane*?

14. What was the killer in *Silver Blaze*?

15. What was the killer in *The Speckled Band*?

16. Name the Duke of Balmoral's horse.

17. What bit off Jonathan Small's right leg?

18. Who owned the dog Pompey?

19. Who was the owner of Silver Blaze?

20. What did Henry Wood call his mongoose?

Inns and Hotels

(Answers To This Quiz Found On Page 94)

There are many different inns and hotels mentioned in the canon. Let's see how well you know some of them:

Who stayed at	Match
1. Anerly Arms	A. Sherlock Holmes and Dr. Watson
2. Bentleys	B. King of Bohemia
3. Madame Charpentiers	C. John Hector McFarlane
4. Dacre Hotel	D. Prince of Colonna
5. Englischer Hof, Baden	E. Jack and Beryl Stapleton
6. Englischer Hof, Meiringen	F. Sir Henry Baskerville
7. Hereford Arms	G. The University of Cambridge rugger team
8. Langham	H. Enoch J. Drebber
9. Nexborough Private Hotel	I. Lady Frances Carfax
10. Northumberland	

On the High Seas

(Answers To This Quiz Found On Page 95)

There are fifteen references to ships in the canon. Identify the ship referred to in the clue given.

Use	Clues
A. Alicia	1. Sailed from Falmouth on October 8, 1855 bound for Australia
B. Aurora	2. Mentioned in *Abbey Grange* (use twice)
C. Bass Rock	3. Mentioned in *The Cardboard Box*
D. Esmeralda	4. Steam launch of Mordecai Smith
E. Friesland	5. Referred to in the canon but so far unpublished (use 4 times)
F. Gloria Scott	6. Mentioned in *The Illustrious Client*
G. Hotspur	7. Besides the Aurora, it is mentioned also in *The Sign of Four*
H. Matilda Briggs	8. Mentioned in *The Valley of Fear*
I. May Day	9. The troopship that carried Watson from India to Portsmouth

J.   Norah Creina

K.   Orontes

L.   Palmyra

M.   Rock of Gibraltar

N.   Ruritania

O.   Sophy Anderson

10.   Mentioned in *The Resident Patient*

11.   Mentioned in *The "Gloria Scott"* (not F)

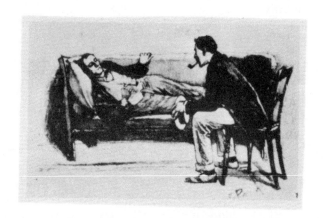

Genius at Work

(Answers To This Quiz Found On Page 96)

When Watson first met Holmes (*A Study in Scarlet*), the good Doctor classified Sherlock's knowledge in twelve specific areas. Fill in the missing word.

Knowledge of:

1. Politics - _____

2. Botany - _____

3. Literature - _____

4. Anatomy - _____

5. Philosophy - _____

6. Chemistry - _____

7. Astronomy - _____

8. Geology - _____

9. Sensational literature - _____

10. Plays the _____ well

11. Is an expert singlestick player, boxer, and _____

12. Has a good practical knowledge of British _____

Note: Many of the inadequacies cited above were subsequently disproved by Holmes.

13. In *The Noble Bachelor* Holmes quotes which American writer's famous remark on circumstantial evidence?

14. In *A Case of Identity* Holmes recognizes a quote from which French writer in one of Hosmer Angel's letters?

15. In *The Sussex Vampire* Holmes alludes to fairy tales by which German authors?

16. In *The Boscombe Valley Mystery* Holmes discourses on which writer?

17. In which case did Holmes use the Bible to clear up a mysterious point?

18. In *The Sign of Four* Holmes quotes twice from which German author?

19. Of which humanistic classic did Holmes say, "Let me recommend this book — one of the most remarkable ever penned."?

20. What was Holmes' *Magnum Opus* of his later years?

21. Which work by Holmes was said to be "the last word" on medieval music by experts in the field?

22. What is the name of the book to which Holmes planned to devote his declining years?

23. Holmes's knowledge of which book was "a trifle rusty"?

24. Which annual almanac did Holmes frequently make use of?

25. In *A Case of Identity* Holmes compares Horace to which other writer?

26. Which Greek writer was Holmes reading on the train in *The Boscombe Valley Mystery*?

27. According to Holmes, the Cornish language might be akin to which ancient language?

28- Name at least 3 of the 5 subjects upon which Holmes dis-
30. coursed in *The Sign of Four*, "handling each as though he had made a special study of it".

Unpublished Cases

(Answers To This Quiz Found On Page 97)

Many of Holmes' cases have never been published. All we have are
the alluring titles. Fill in the missing word.

1. The Singular Affair of the _____ Crutch

2. The _____ Poisoning Case

3. The Sudden Death of Cardinal _____

4. The _____ Patriarchs

5. The Repulsive Story of the Red _____

6. The Giant _____ of Sumatra

7. The _____ Murder in Odessa

8. The _____ Chamber

9. The Politician, the Lighthouse and the Trained _____ _____

10. _____ of the Club-Foot and His Abominable
    Wife

11. Vanderbilt and the _____

12. The Dreadful Business of the Abernetty Family of _____ _____

13. _____ , the Wine Merchant

14. The Adventure of the Old _____ Woman

15. The _____ Substitution Scandal

16. The Adventure of the Amateur _____ Society

17. Bert Stevens, the Terrible _____

18. The _____ Separation Case

19. The Fate of Victor _____

20. The _____ Jewel Case

21. The _____ Will Case

22. The Abbas _____ Tragedy

23. The Atrocious Conduct of Colonel _____

24. The Adventure of the Tired _____

25. The Bogus _____ Affair

26. The _____ of Colonel Carruthers

27. Colonel Warburton's _____

28. The Capture of Archie Stamford, the _____

29. Morgan, the _____

30. The arrest of Wilson, the Notorious _____

31. The _____ Lizard

32. Vigor, the Hammersmith _____

33. Vittoria, the Circus _____

34. The Mortal _____ of Old Abrahams

35. The Commission for the Sultan of _____

Words of Wisdom I

(Answers To This Quiz Found On Pages 98-100)

Fill in the missing word(s) from these statements of the Master.

1. There is nothing in which deduction is so necessary as in _____ .

2. There is but one step from the grotesque to the _____ _____ .

3. I am the last and highest court of appeal in _____ .

4. Our highest assurance of the goodness of _____ seems to me to rest in the flowers.

5. ...when you have eliminated the impossible, whatever remains, however _____ , must be the truth.

6. Here is my lens. You know my _____ .

7. It is a capital mistake to theorize before one has _____ _____ .

8. It is of the highest importance in the art of detection to be able to recognize, out of a number of facts, which are incidental and which _____ .

9. The more _____ a thing is, the less mysterious it proves to be.

10. The more outrè and grotesque an incident is, the more carefully it deserves to be _____ .

11. I get a wife out of it, Jones gets the credit; pray what remains for you?" "For me," said Sherlock Holmes, "there still remains the _____ .

12. I read nothing except the _____ news and the. . . .

13. _____ column.

14. My Biblical knowledge is a trifle _____ .

15. My mind is like a _____ , tearing itself to pieces. . . .

16. My professional charges are upon a _____ .

17. You have a grand gift of _____ Watson. It makes you quite

18. invaluable as a _____ .

19. The horse is a very _____ creature.

20. . . . there is nothing so unnatural as the _____ .

21. I suppose that I am committing a felony, but it is just possible that I am saving a _____ . . . besides, it is the season

22. of _____ .

23. The ways of _____ are indeed hard to understand.

24. If there is not some _____ hereafter, then the world is a

25. cruel _____ .

26. The example of patient _____ is in itself the most precious

27. of all lessons to an _____ world.

28. Is not all life pathetic and _____ ?

29. To a great mind, nothing is _____ .

30. Where there is no _____ there is no horror.

31. The world is big enough for us. No _____ need apply.

32. One's ideas must be as broad as _____ .

33. . . . I have trained myself to see what others _____ .

34. I think of writing another little monograph some of these days on the _____ and its relation to crime.

35. _____ is almost invariably a clue.

36. _____ evidence is a very tricky thing.

37. It is always awkward doing business with an _____ .

38. I am not retained by the police to supply their _____ _____ .

39. Crime is _____ .

40. _____ is rare.

41. . . . the lowest and vilest alleys of London do not present a more dreadful record of sin than does its smiling and beautiful _____ .

42. . . . the deduction of a man's _____ from his writing is one which has been brought to considerable accuracy by experts.

43. The faculty of deduction is certainly _____ .

44. I can _____ facts, Watson, but I cannot

45. _____ them.

46. Women are naturally _____ .

47. One should always look for a possible _____ and provide against it. It is the

48. _____ rule of criminal investigation.

49. I think there are certain crimes which the law cannot touch and which therefore, to some extent, justify private _____ _____ .

50. I choose to be only associated with those crimes which present some _____ in their solution.

51. A _____ mind – all great criminals have that.

52. When you follow two separate chains of _____ you will find some point of

53. _____ which should approximate to the truth.

54. I never make _____ .

55. There's the _____ thread of murder running through the

56. _____ skein of life, and our duty is to

57. _____ it, and isolate it and expose every

58. _____ of it.

59. There is no branch of detective science which is so important and so much neglected as the art of _____

60. _____ .

61. There is nothing more stimulating than a case where _____
_____ goes against you.

62. You can tell an old master by the _____ of his
brush. I can tell a

63. _____ when I see one.

64. The motives of women are so _____ .

65. Woman's heart and mind are _____ puzzles to
the male.

66. One of the most dangerous classes in the world is the _____
_____ and friendless woman.

67. Women are never to be entirely _____ .

68. I should never marry myself, lest I _____ my
judgment.

69. What you do in this world is a matter of no _____
____ .

70. _____ are occasionally of extraordinary interest.

71. The _____ , Watson, is a most valuable institu-
tion if you only know how to use it.

72. A dog reflects the _____ life.

73. _____ don't make mistakes.

74. I would rather have _____'s help than that of
the whole detective force in London.

75. Let us escape from this weary workaday world by the side door of _____ .

76. A study of family _____ is enough to convert a man to the

77. doctrine of _____ .

78. The _____ is a paper which is seldom found in any hands but

79. those of the highly _____ .

80. . . . off to _____ land, where all is sweetness and delicacy and harmony.

81. There is a strong family resemblance about _____ .

82. Everything comes in circles, even _____ .

83. You can file it in our _____ , Watson.

84. The most _____ crime is often the most mysterious. . .

85. Never trust to general impressions, but concentrate yourself upon _____ .

86. Detection is, as ought to be, an exact _____ .

87. There is nothing like first-hand _____ .

88. _____ evidence is a very tricky thing.

89. _____ never ends. It is a series of lessons, with the greatest for the last.

90. The _____ qualities are antagonistic to clear reasoning.

91. When a doctor goes wrong he is the _____ of criminals.

92. Chess — one mark of a _____ mind.

93. The faculties become refined when you _____ them.

94. Some people without possessing genius have a remarkable power of _____ it.

95. Good old Watson! You are the one fixed point in a _____ age.

96. We approached the case with an absolutely _____ mind, which is almost an advantage.

97. A man should keep his little brain _____ stocked with all the

98. _____ he is likely to use.

99. Everyone has some little _____ spark concealed about him.

100. Work is the best antidote to _____ .

Words of Wisdom II

(Answers To This Quiz Found On Pages 100-101)

101. There is nothing so _____ as the commonplace.

102. It's a _____ world.

103. The most difficult crime to track is the one which is _____ .

104. It is stupidity rather than _____ to refuse to recognize danger when it is close upon you.

105. Do nothing _____ .

106. The _____'s agents may be of flesh and blood.

107. A _____ gets no credit when once he has explained his trick.

108. Be precise as to _____ .

109. It is as well to _____ everything.

110. The gestures are given to man as the means by which he shall express his _____ .

111. What a lovely thing a _____ is.

112. What one man can invent another can _____ .

113. It is only an amiable man in this world who receives _____ _____ .

114. The world is full of things which nobody by any chance ever _____ .

115. How often is _____ the mother of truth?

116. The resources of _____ are far from being exhausted.

117. The _____ place that has once been used may be again.

118. _____ are common to all mortals, and the greatest is he who can recognize and repair them.

119. Let us get a firm grip on the very little which we do know, so that when fresh _____ arise we may be ready to fit them into their pieces.

120. Some people's affability is more deadly than the _____ _____ of coarser souls.

121. We all have neglected _____ to deplore.

122. A certain selection and discretion must be used in producing a _____ effect.

123. One has to be _____ when one talks of high matters of state.

124. Grasp the _____ , Watson!

125. An exception disproves the _____ .

126. Circumstantial evidence is occasionally very _____ .

127. Things must be done _____ and in order.

128. Evidence taken on the spot has a _____ value.

129. When the other fellow has all the _____ , it saves time to throw down your hand.

130. _____ business men don't conceal their place of business.

131. It is simpler to deal _____ .

132. There are times when a brutal frontal _____ is the best policy.

133. You do occasionally find a carrion crow among the _____ _____ .

134. We must _____ while the iron is hot.

135. There is nothing so important as _____ .

136. There is nothing more deceptive than an obvious _____
    _____ .

137. Make a point of never having any _____ , and
    of following docilely wherever fact may lead.

138. It is necessary that the _____ should be able
    to utilize all the facts which have come to his knowledge.

139. What a man may do in the _____ is a hard
    question to answer.

140. You never know what turn _____ might take.

141. _____ begat contempt.

142. It is human to _____ .

143. Human nature is a _____ mixture.

144. How dangerous it always is to reason from _____
    data.

145. This is our _____ , for it begins in defeat and
    ends in victory.

146. All _____ comes useful to the detective.

147. All sorts of _____ knowledge comes useful.

148. It is not what we know, but what we can _____ .

149. The _____ of ideas and the oblique uses of
    knowledge

150. are often of _____ interest.

Sir Arthur Conan Doyle

(Answers To This Quiz Found On Page 102)

1. When was Doyle born?

2. From which university did he receive his M.A. in 1881 and M.D. in 1885?

3. Which political office did Doyle unsuccessfully seek 3 times?

4. In which religion was he born and reared?

5. Which religion did he profess in his later years?

6. Which famous Jesuit school did he attend?

7. Where was Doyle practicing medicine when he published *A Study in Scarlet*?

8. When was he knighted?

9. Where was Doyle living when he wrote the first short stories?

10. Whom did Doyle marry in 1907?

11. In 1909 Doyle wrote a booklet exposing government persecution and exploitation of the people of which country?

12. From 1911 to 1927 Doyle undertook almost singlehandedly the case of a man wrongfully convicted of murder. Who was he?

13. Who was Doyle's first wife?

Doyle wrote a number of other books. Can you match the description on the left with the correct title?

14. A defense of the British   A. The Exploits of Brigadier
    Army in South Africa   Gerard

15. A tale of Monmouth's   B. Micah Clarke
    rebellion

16. A romance of DuGuesclin's   C. Cause and Conduct of the
    time   World War

17. A series of stories of   D. History of Spiritualism
    the Napoleonic Wars

18. A propaganda tract   E. Rodney Stone

19. A religious apologia   F. The Great Boer War

20. A sketch about prize-   G. The White Company
    fighting in the days of
    the Prince Regent

The Scions

(Answers To This Quiz Found On Page 103)

Sherlockian enthusiasts all over the world have gathered in groups to promote study of and reverence for the Sacred Writings. See if you can match the proper scion society with the city in which it is located.

Societies	Cities
1. The Amateur Mendicant Society	A. Ontario, Canada
2.* The Baker Street Irregulars	B. Tokyo
3. The Baker Street Pageboys	C. Detroit
4. The Baker Street Squires	D. Atlanta
5. The Bald-Headed Men	E. Cleveland
6. The Baritsu Society	F. Providence
7. The Briony Lodgers	G. Westchester County, N.Y.
8. The Confederates of Wisteria Lodge	H. New York City
9. The Creeping Men	I. Indianapolis
10. The Dancing Men	J. Lincoln, Neb.
11. The Five Orange Pips	K. Los Angeles
12. The Illustrious Clients	L. Great Neck, L.I., N.Y.
13. The Napoleons of Crime	M. Milwaukee

*   Properly called "sister" societies rather than scions.

14. The Norwegian Explorers   N.   Sydney, Australia

15. The Red Circle   O.   Baltimore

16. The Red-Headed League   P.   Philadelphia

17.* The Sherlock Holmes   Q.   London
Society

18. The Six Napoleons   R.   Wellesley Hills, Mass.

19. The Sons of the Copper   S.   Washington, D.C.
Beeches

20. The Speckled Band   T.   St. Paul

*   Properly called "sister" societies rather than scions.

Miscellany I

(Answers To This Quiz Found On Pages 104-105)

1. Who said "I hear of Sherlock everywhere"?

2. Why would a knowledge of ophiology be helpful in *The Speckled Band*?

3. Whose left ear was a distinguishing feature?

4. Who died the night after his capture of a burst aortic aneurism?

5. What did Holmes have a horror of destroying?

6. How much of his wound pension did Watson spend on racing?

7. What did Holmes call the "countries of assassination"?

8. In which case does Dr. Ray Ernest appear?

9. What directory of clergymen did Holmes use to look up Rev. J. C. Elman?

10. Who wore gray-tinted glasses and a large Masonic pin?

11. Who was "a misshapen demon with a soul as distorted as his body"?

12. What did both Holmes and Watson "have a weakness for"?

13. Who was "a huge, coarse, red faced, scorbutic man with a pair of vivid black eyes"?

14. Which famous mystery novelist and critic founded an early scion society, The San Francisco Scowrers?

15. To which of his relatives was Holmes referring when he said: "Art in the blood is liable to take the strangest forms"?

16. Irish coal miners in Pennsylvania appear in which case?

17. What profession did Irene Adler follow?

18. In the early 1950s an apochryphal Holmes story was supposedly "discovered" but later found to be an imitation. Do you remember its name?

19. What flower did Mrs. Stapleton ask Watson to pick for her on the moor?

20. Who was the physician upon whom Doyle modeled Holmes?

21. *A Study in Scarlet* appeared in which magazine in 1887?

22. Which American magazine first published a Sherlock Holmes story?

23. In which British magazine did most of the stories subsequently appear?

24. Who did early portraits of Holmes and the characters in the cases for *The Strand*?

25. What was the name of the gang of street arabs who assisted Holmes on a number of occasions?

26. Who was the long-suffering landlady of 221B?

27. When was the Sherlock Holmes Society of London founded?

28-29. Which two American Presidents were members of the Baker Street Irregulars?

30. In which New York restaurant did the first Baker Street Irregulars' dinner occur in 1934?

31. Which case occurs near Christmas and contains a Christmas goose?

32. While Holmes would be reading or writing monographs, Watson would often be reading what?

33. Watson's wound (or wounds) came from which war?

34. Who burst into 221B and promptly fainted on the hearth-rug?

35. Where is the "Sherlock Holmes" pub located in London (give street)?

36. The three year period between *The Final Problem* and *The Empty House* has been called _____ .

37. Most Sherlockians accept which date (year) as Holmes's birthday? Why?

38. Can you name the Oxford Street tobacconist which supplied Holmes with strong shag and Watson with cigarettes?

39. What did Holmes call the "lighthouses of the future"?

40. Whose circus was in competition with Wombwell and Ronder in *The Veiled Lodger*?

Without getting into complex, interminable arguments about chronology, let's match the month given by Watson in the canon with the case to which it refers.

41. The second morning after Christmas   A.   The Crooked Man

42. One morning in June   B.   The Final Problem

43. One summer night, a few months after my marriage   C.   The Resident Patient

44. 24 April-4 May, 1891   D.   The Stockbroker's Clerk

45. A gloomy February   E.   Charles Augustus
     morning   Milverton

46. It had been a close,   F.   The Missing Three-
     rainy day in October   Quarter

47. It was after tea on a   G.   The Abbey Grange
     summer evening

48. Holmes and I . . . had   H.   The Golden Pince-Nez
     returned about six o'clock
     on a cold, frosty winter's
     evening

49. It was a wild tempestuous   I.   The Greek Interpreter
     night, towards the close
     of November

50. It was on a bitterly cold   J.   The Blue Carbuncle
     night and frosty morning
     towards the end of the
     winter

Miscellany II

(Answers To This Quiz Found On Pages 106-107)

1. Who wrote a treatise on the coptic monasteries in Egypt?

2. In which bank in Charing Cross is kept a dispatch box containing additional case records of Holmes and Watson?

3. Who was Holmes' source of information about the London underworld?

4. What does Holmes call "our highest assurance of the goodness of Providence"?

5. Who wrote "I will be at Thor Bridge at nine o'clock"?

6. To whom was it written?

7. Who was the clown in the Ronder Circus?

8. Who wrote *Heavy Game of the Western Himalayas*?

9. Of which church was Mrs. Barclay (in *The Crooked Man*) a member?

10. A genuine painting by whom hung in Thaddeus Sholto's home?

11. Whom did Holmes call "the stormy petrel of crime"?

12. Who was Holmes' only close friend at college?

13. Who was murdered at Abbey Grange?

14. Who was the Harley Street specialist who advised Holmes to rest or have a complete breakdown (in *The Devil's Foot*)?

15. Who was the distinguished physician that Watson wanted to bring in to examine Holmes (in *The Dying Detective*)?

16. According to Watson in *The Dying Detective*, who was the greatest living authority on tropical diseases?

17. Who was Anna's true love in *The Golden Pince-Nez*?

18. Who was the proprietor of the Green Dragon Inn at Crendall?

19. Who was J. Neil Gibson's estate manager?

20. Who wrote "The Book of Life"?

21. Where did Holmes generally keep his tobacco?

22. In 1954 the BBC produced a classic series of cases from the canon. Do you remember who played Holmes?

23. Who played Watson?

24. Who played Moriarty in *The Final Problem*?

25. What did Holmes use to revive Watson after the latter's fainting spell?

26. Dr. Grimesby Roylott once practiced medicine in which Indian city?

27. Whose "sudden death" did Holmes investigate "at the express desire of the Pope"?

28. For whom did Jonathan Harker work?

29. Baron Gruner was a recognized authority on what subject?

30. Holmes admired Norman Neruda's playing of a piece by which composer?

31. Who liberated Lucknow in the Indian Mutiny?

32. The black pearl disappeared from whose bedroom?

33. Oberstein used the agony column of which newspaper to get the secret documents?

34-36. Can you name three of "The Four"?

37. Who was the intolerant fiance of Lady Eva Blackwell?

38. Who wrote "Dynamics of an Asteroid"?

39. Who was the vicar at Little Purlington?

40. Soon after his marriage, Watson bought a practice from whom?

41. Who owned the Three Gables prior to Mary Maberley?

42. Of what nationality was Mme. Henri Fournaye?

43. Whom did Holmes call "the Austrian murderer"?

44. Who was the surly innkeeper of the Fighting Cock Inn?

45. Who was Percy Phelps' uncle?

46. Who was the plumber accused of taking the blue carbuncle?

47. Who appears as landlady for Holmes and Watson only in *A Scandal in Bohemia*?

48. Charles Gorot was of which religious descent?

49. Who was Mr. Oldacre's tailor?

50. Who took over Watson's practice while he and Holmes went to Aldershot in *The Crooked Man*?

51. Who was the senior clerk at Woolwich Arsenal?

52. What award did Holmes win for his arrest of Huret?

53. Who was the strong man of the Ronder circus?

54. Who was a librarian friend of Watson who helped Watson select a volume on Chinese pottery?

55. Who was an evil influence on James Ryder?

Miscellany III

(Answers To This Quiz Found On Pages 107-109)

1.   Whose blue carbuncle was stolen?

2-3.   Which two drugs did Holmes occasionally use?

4.   Who had a pawn shop in Westminster Road?

5.   Who was a violin virtuoso as well as a criminal?

6.   In an unpublished case, who stepped back into his home to get an umbrella and "was never more seen in this world"?

7.   Who was J. Neil Gibson's Brazilian wife?

8.   Who was killed by a poisoned dart?

9.   Who was slain in Waterloo Road by "killer" Evans?

10.   Who was the wooden-legged grocer in *The Beryl Coronet*?

11.   Who was the vicar in *The Devil's Foot*?

12.   Who was the Duke of Holdernesse's son?

13.   Who wrote *Sidelights on Horace*?

14.   Who was principal of the Theological College of St. George's?

15.   Who had a "face burned yellow with the sun and marked by every evil passion"?

16.   Which London theatre revived the play *Sherlock Holmes* in the 1973-1974 season?

17.   Which city's library has a magnificent Sherlockian collection?

18. In which year was a Sherlock Holmes exhibition presented at the Festival of Britain?

19. Which English publisher first brought out an omnibus volume of the complete canon?

20. Which illustrator produced the deer-stalker?

21. Which illustrator produced the curved pipe?

22. With what instrument did Holmes transfix unanswered correspondence to the mantelshelf?

23. Whom does Holmes clobber with his revolver butt in *The Three Garridebs*?

24. What did Watson call "ineffable twaddle"?

25. Who gave Holmes an emerald pin?

26. What was the name of a collection of pastiches written by Adrian Conan Doyle and John Dickson Carr, published in 1954?

27. Who was "the fourth smartest man in London"?

28. During which battle was Watson wounded?

29. At which base hospital did he recover?

30. What disease did he catch?

31. What kind of bullet struck his arm (and/or leg)?

32. Who is the mysterious person that Sherlockians often blame for apparent inconsistencies or contradictions in the canon?

33. What was the seven per cent solution?

34. How often did Holmes use it in *The Sign of Four*?

35. Who typed all of his letters, even his signature?

36. Who gave a snuff box to Holmes?

37. What does Dorothy Sayers believe Watson's middle name to be?

38. Who wore a "Scotch bonnet" on his visit to Baker Street?

39. To whom was Holmes referring when he said "When a doctor goes wrong, he is the first of criminals"?

40. In *The Noble Bachelor*, Watson refers to a letter Holmes received from a tide-waiter. What is a tide-waiter?

Violet is a popular first name in the canon. Name the Violet who appeared in these cases:

41. The Copper Beeches

42. The Solitary Cyclist

43. The Bruce-Partington Plans

44. The Illustrious Client

45. Who took Watson's practice for a few days in *The Boscombe Valley Mystery*?

46. What's the weather like at the opening of *The Cardboard Box*?

47. Who was a "giggling ruffian" and "a man of the foulest antecedents"?

48. At the end of *The Greek Interpreter* "a curious newspaper cutting" reached Holmes and Watson. Where did it come from?

49. Who was the blind German mechanic in *The Empty House*?

50. Who was "preparing a map of the Holy Land, with special reference to the kingdom of the Midianites, upon which he was writing a monograph"?

51. During Holmes' three year absence, who kept the rooms at 221B intact?

52. Who attempted suicide in *The Retired Colourman*?

53. Susan Stockdale appears in which case?

The Higher Criticism
(Answers To This Quiz Found On Page 110)

Thousands of books, essays, and articles have been written about the Sherlock Holmes saga. Commentaries on the Sacred Writings are indispensable for the serious Sherlockian. Every true aficionado of the canon should be able to name the authors of the following classics:

1. The Sherlock Holmes Companion

2. My Dear Holmes

3. The Late Mr. Sherlock Holmes

4. The London of Sherlock Holmes

5. The Private Life of Sherlock Holmes

6. Sherlock Holmes of Baker Street: A Life of the World's First Consulting Detective

7. Holmes and Watson: A Miscellany

8. A Sherlock Holmes Commentary

9. In the Footsteps of Sherlock Holmes

10. The Annotated Sherlock Holmes

11. Baker Street Byways

12. Sherlock Holmes, Fact or Fiction?

13. An Irregular Guide to Sherlock Holmes

14. Watson was a Woman

15. Studies in the Literature of Sherlock Holmes

16.   Sherlock Holmes and the Pygmies

17.   Ex Libris Sherlock Holmes

18.   Dr. Watson's Christian Name

19.   Who edited a 1944 anthology of parodies and pastiches entitled *The Misadventures of Sherlock Holmes*?

20.   Who wrote the classic preface, "In Memoriam Sherlock Holmes," to the original two-volume omnibus published by Doubleday in 1930?

21.   Who wrote *Sherlock Holmes and Music*?

22.   Who wrote "Holmes and Watson still live for all that love them well — in a romantic chamber of the heart, in a nostalgic country of the mind where it is always 1895"?

23.   Who wrote the first scholarly investigation of the canon and can be said to have inaugurated Sherlockian studies?

24.   Who wrote *A Doctor Enjoys Sherlock Holmes*?

25.   Who collected a series of introductions to the saga entitled *Introducing Mr. Sherlock Holmes*?

26-29.   Which four cases does Martin Dakin reject as spurious and non-canonical?

30.   Which Sherlockian commentator claimed that Holmes committed suicide after he realized he was going blind?

There are a number of theories concerning Holmes's exploits during his hiatus. Can you match the theory with its author?

31. Holmes murdered Moriarty and disappeared until the case blew over.

a. Martin Dakin

b. Anthony Boucher

32. Holmes lived with Irene Adler in Montenegro.

c. Gavin Brend

d. William Baring-Gould

33. Holmes joined the Moriarty gang and undermined them from within.

e. W.S. Bristowe

34. Holmes really died at the falls but was replaced by a cousin and double Sherrinford Holmes.

35. Holmes suffered from a serious loss of memory.

The Distaff Side

(Answers To This Quiz Found On Page 111)

In which case do each of the following ladies appear?

1.	Irene Adler	16.	Mary Maberley
2.	Anna	17.	Violet De Merville
3.	Maud Bellamy	18.	Flora Millar
4.	Lady Brackenstall	19.	Mary Morstan
5.	Miss Burnet	20.	Lucy Parr
6.	Elsie Cubitt	21.	Eugenia Ronder
7.	Sarah Cushing	22.	Ettie Shafter
8.	Marie Devine	23.	Violet Smith
9.	Dolores	24.	Helen Stoner
10.	Hatty Doran	25.	Mary Sutherland
11.	Grace Dunbar	26.	Brenda Tregennis
12.	Rachel Howells	27.	Mrs. Warren
13.	Violet Hunter	28.	Violet Westbury
14.	Isadora Klein	29.	Kitty Winter
15.	Laura Lyons	30.	Theresa Wright

The Constabulary

(Answers To This Quiz Found On Page 112)

Holmes' dazzling brilliance frequently puts members of the constabulary to shame. On a few rare occasions, an inspector here and there will show some promise. Let's see how well you know these inspectors and constables.

Match the inspector on the right with the case in which he appears. They may be used several times.

1.	The Resident Patient	a.	Gregson
2.	The Boscombe Valley Mystery	b.	Lanner
3.	The Six Napoleons	c.	Lestrade
4.	The Bruce Partington Plans	d.	Forbes
5.	The Naval Treaty	e.	MacDonald
6.	The Valley of Fear	f.	Hopkins
7.	Wisteria Lodge	g.	Bradstreet
8.	The Norwood Builder		
9.	The Noble Bachelor		
10.	The Red Circle		
11.	Black Peter		
12.	The Man with the Twisted Lip		
13.	The Blue Carbuncle		

14. The Golden Pince-Nez

15. The Engineers Thumb

16. The Missing Three Quarter

17. Abbey Grange

18. Charles Augustus Milverton

_____

19. Whom did Holmes call "the smartest of the Scotland Yard-ers" in *A Study in Scarlet*?

20. What kind of accent did Inspector Alec MacDonald have?

21. Who was the Surrey constable that Holmes said had instinct and intuition?

22. In which case did Inspector Forrester appear?

23. Who was "the little detective; a small wiry bulldog of a man"?

24. Athelney Jones appears in only one case. Which?

25. Which inspector appears in the largest number of cases?

All Numbers

(Answers To This Quiz Found On Page 113)

Fill in the missing number.

1. The _____ Garridebs.

2. The Sign of _____ .

3. The _____ Napoleons.

4. The _____ Gables.

5. The _____ Orange Pips.

6. The _____ Students.

7. How many short stories are there in the canon?

8. How many novels or novellas?

9. How many steps lead up to the sitting room at 221B?

10. How much did Holmes pay for his stradivarius in Tottenham Court Road?

11. According to the opening sentence in *The Veiled Lodger*, how many years were Holmes and Watson associated in detection?

12. How many brothers did Moriarty have?

13. How much did the Duke of Holdernesse pay Holmes for his services?

14. What was Sir James Damery's private telephone number?

15. For how much did Conan Doyle sell *A Study in Scarlet* in 1887?

16.   How many years older than Sherlock was Mycroft?

17.   With how many tobacco ashes was Holmes familiar?

18.   How many different tire impressions did Holmes know?

19.   With how many perfumes was Holmes familiar?

20.   Holmes had at least how many refuges in London where he could hide or put on a disguise?

Nicknames and Aliases

(Answers To This Quiz Found On Page 114)

I have listed the nicknames or aliases of several characters from the canon. Can you supply the real names?

1. Hargrave

2. Black Peter

3. Porky

4. Black Jack of Ballarat

5. Pierrot

6. Cornelius

7. Vincent Spaulding

8. Fritz

9. William Darbyshire

10. Altamont

11. Holy Peters

12. Killer Evans

13. Sigerson

14. Jem

15. Tiger of San Pedro

16. Who was "The worst man in London . . . the king of all the blackmailers"?

17. Who was "The second most dangerous man in London"?

18. Who was "The Napoleon of crime"?

19. What is the nom de plume of an informer employed by Holmes in *The Valley of Fear*?

20. Who was Black Jack?

Born to the Purple

(Answers To This Quiz Found On Page 114)

Members of the nobility appear with frequency in the canon. Can you fill in the missing title, i.e. "Lord", "Sir", "Baron", etc. for these characters?

1. _____ Henry Baskerville

2. _____ Bellinger

3. _____ Cantlemere

4. _____ Adelbert Gruner

5. _____ of Holdernesse

6. _____ Holdhurst

7. _____ Mount-James

8. _____ Robert Norberton

9. _____ Robert St. Simon

10. _____ Arthur Saltire

11. _____ Negretto Sylvius

12. _____ Von Herling

13. _____ James Walter

14. _____ Eustace Brackenstall

15. _____ Cathcart Soames

Sherlockian Scramble

(Answers To This Quiz Found On Pages 115-117)

No quiz book would be complete without at least one scramble. You are to deduce the correct place, name or character from the mishmash below.

1.	RADLEOON	17.	VTRIMLENO
2.	AIOGGNRO	18.	DORERN
3.	HGITILCSR	19.	TEDLSRNAE
4.	KNSGTEINON	20.	ERGAIET
5.	ANERSUDS	21.	ITRAIWSE
6.	OTETNSUHRO	22.	ONV OBKR
7.	TAETSPLNO	23.	HESISLSNREG
8.	CULCA RNEGNAO	24.	OSLTHO
9.	OESEINLWNT	25.	OOHHAK
10.	ANNA BASHI	26.	BDEBRRE
11.	UGAEMSRV	27.	UHTXBALE
12.	IRTOPER	28.	YROGDFE ONTORN
13.	ANOBR UCIVER	29.	LCKBA WSNA
14.	ATMDRORO	30.	RDSIAOA ILKEN
15.	TELYAHHRE	31.	WINAKR
16.	RNRGUE	32.	UALP SKTEIRAD

33. YRTFMCO

34. ASNWTO

35. KMRREA

36. OYAETMRLN

37. EADSYMUL

38. WERIMRLO

39. NINHPCI ALEN

40. NIPNRE

41. NRHSTUTO

42. BDRAGRIE

43. RTIVCO RVRTEO

44. ETWYWSAA

45. ETILEWSUL RASM

46. OLIWLIMASN

47. NAWDMIA

48. YOMABB

49. YLOSBBOMUR

50. TLCHABAKEH

51. NHRGCAI SORCS

52. EITTB

53. ZFHAI

54. UULSRIILTOS NICLET

55. TLRMBEBAEY TOHLE

56. SEREDLTA

57. RTEIELCSE

58. JNSAO ALOCEDR

59. IVTRCO YLHCN

60. RALUA SNYLO

61. ARMY TORAMSN

62. AAVLN RAYTET

63. SUSXES RIMAVPE

64. EDNSLE

65. ESEILL TOKSOAHT

66. SDSAOE

67. SEHWPARU

68. ARSNPEO

69. SERINPA EILSPPR

70. SDHONU

71. SEEILDPTRFE

72. POYPME

73. SEIONDGE ULCB	87. TMSORHEW
74. SUSNA YBODNE	88. EIRDRTE AOCORMLUN
75. NAI HORUMDC	89. LUBE NABCRUECL
76. LCROA	90. LBULADHA NHKA
77. NNUCNIGAMH	91. EASX-RUOCBG RQSAEU
78. EASJM ROMIERTM	92. NOETNILWSE
79. YTOIAMRR	93. EAELMBRY
80. RDGAEWE ORDA	94. AZAMRIN OTSEN
81. IRYBD SADEWRD	95. BIEHNHCRCEA LAFLS
82. NDMTNEOO ERSTET	96. IIOETRCLT
83. LREIKL NVEAS	97. EHOJPR TAURCSEL
84. LSMRAEEDA	98. AOTEMHM ISHNG
85. NISREEGLH OFH	99. OMISPSN
86. UTOESN ITSATON	100. SIGRSEON

Scoring

90-100 — Super

80-89 — Good Show

65-79 — O.K.

0-64 — Well??

Colours

(Answers To This Quiz Found On Page 118)

What colour is referred to in these questions?

1. The _____ Circle

2. A Study in _____

3. The _____ Carbuncle

4. The _____ Face

5. The Five _____ Pips

6. The _____-headed League

7. _____ Blaze

8. _____ Peter

9-11. What three colours are mentioned in reference to Holmes' dressing gowns?

12. The _____ Bull Inn (near the Priory School)

13. _____ King. (He granted the Birlstone estate to Hugo de Capus)

14. Silas _____ (manager of Mapleton)

15. Admiral _____ (commanded the Sea of Azov fleet in the Crimean War)

16. Josiah _____ (his bust of Napoleon was stolen by Beppo)

17. _____ Dragon (an inn three miles from Shoscombe Old Place)

18. _____ Swan Hotel (Violet Hunter wanted to consult Holmes here)

19. _____'s Inn Road (Holmes and Watson were enroute to King's Cross Station in *The Missing Three-Quarter*)

20. _____ Tor (Holmes hid here in disguise in *The Hound of the Baskervilles*)

The Hired Help
(Answers To This Quiz Found On Page 119)

This little quiz is all about maids, butlers and other supportive personnel who appear at times in the canon. See how well you know them.

1. Who was Holmes's pageboy in *The Mazarin Stone*?

2. Who was the leader of the Baker Street Irregulars, "an urchin of no fixed abode"?

3. Who was Holmes' "general utility man"?

4. Who was Mr. and Mrs. John Douglas's butler?

5. Who was the maid that brought Ned Hunter his supper?

6. Who was Mrs. Ferguson's maid in *The Sussex Vampire*?

7. Who was Professor Coram's secretary?

8. Who was Mrs. Cunningham's coachman?

9. Who was Professor Presbury's coachman?

10. Who was the incorrigible maid that Mary Morstan Watson fired?

11. Who was the stablehand at the Ferguson estate in Sussex?

12. Who was Eduardo Lucas' valet?

13. Who was Professor Coram's gardener, "an old Crimean man"?

14. Who was Colonel Emsworth's butler?

15. Who was the butler in *The Hound of the Baskervilles*?

16. Who was Lady Beatrice Folder's butler?

17. Name the West End agency that specialized in governesses.

18. Who was the maid in Professor Coram's household?

19. Who was Lady Brackenstall's maid?

20. Who was Lady Beatrice Folder's maid?

On Stage and Screen

(Answers To This Quiz Found On Page 120)

1. What British actor portrayed Holmes in almost 50 films during the 1920s and 1930s?

2. Which great ballet company presented a Sherlock Holmes ballet "The Great Detective" in 1953?

3. What famous Canadian actor played Holmes in the 1931 film "The Speckled Band"?

4. Who played Holmes in *The Return of Sherlock Holmes* (1929) and *Sherlock Holmes* (1933)?

5. Who played Holmes in the 1939 *Hound of the Baskervilles*?

6. Who played Holmes in the 1959 *Hound of the Baskervilles*?

7. Who played Holmes in the 1959 BBC radio series?

8. What was the name of the scandalous, controversial 1971 film about Sherlock Holmes?

9. Who played Holmes in (8) above?

10. Who directed?

11. Name the 1965 Broadway hit show about Sherlock Holmes.

12. Who played Holmes in (11) above?

13. Who played Holmes in a 1922 film "Moriarty"?

14. Who played Billy the pageboy in the play *Sherlock Holmes* in London in 1905?

15. Who played Holmes so well in films and plays during the early 30s that Lady Conan Doyle personally commended him?

16. What American actor wrote and starred in a smash hit play *Sherlock Holmes* in the early days of this century?

17. Who played Dr. Watson in the 1939 *Hound of the Basker-villes*?

18-19. Can you name the two Sherlock Holmes films which appeared in 1933?

20. Who played Holmes in one of them and Watson in the other?

Food and Drink

(Answers To This Quiz Found On Page 121)

1. In which case did Holmes go three days without food or drink?

2. What wine did Holmes and Watson drink in *His Last Bow*?

3. Which famous restaurant in The Strand did Holmes and Watson often frequent?

4. Of what does Holmes say "I never needed it more" in *The Dying Detective*?

5. In which case does a cook mysteriously appear at 221B?

6. What did she serve Holmes and Watson for breakfast?

7. What did Holmes serve Athelney Jones for dinner?

8. In which case does Holmes return a missing document at breakfast, under cover of a dish?

9. Who joined Holmes and Watson for a "quite epicurean little cold supper" at 221B in *The Noble Bachelor*?

10. In referring to Mrs. Hudson, Holmes said that she had "as good an idea of" what as a Scotchwoman? (*The Naval Treaty*)

11. What did the landlady "babble of" in *The Three Students*?

Colonels

(Answers To This Quiz Found On Page 121)

Colonels come off rather poorly as characters in the canon. Most are evil or, at the least, unsympathetic characters. Can you match these prominent colonels with the case in which each appears?

1.	Hayter	A.	The Final Problem
2.	Sebastian Moran	B.	The Bruce-Partington Plans
3.	Moriarty	C.	The Blanched Soldier
4.	James Barclay	D.	Silver Blaze
5.	Valentine Walter	E.	The Hound of the Baskervilles
6.	Carruthers	F.	The Reigate Squires
7.	Upwood	G.	The Copper Beeches
8.	Ross	H.	Wisteria Lodge
9.	Spence Munro	I.	The Crooked Man
10.	Emsworth	J.	The Empty House

ANSWERS

Who's Who

Answers

1. The Reigate Squires
2. The Empty House
3. The Retired Colourman
4. The Valley of Fear
5. A Case of Identity
6. The Missing Three-Quarter
7. The Blue Carbuncle
8. The Valley of Fear
9. The Three Students
10. The Crooked Man
11. The Valley of Fear
12. Wisteria Lodge
13. The Stockbroker's Clerk
14. The Creeping Man
15. The Six Napoleons
16. The Resident Patient
17. The Man with the Twisted Lip
18. The Blue Carbuncle
19. The Six Napoleons
20. Silver Blaze
21. The Cardboard Box
22. The Musgrave Ritual
23. Black Peter
24. Black Peter
25. The Solitary Cyclist
26. The Hound of the Baskervilles
27. A Study in Scarlet
28. The Golden Pince-Nez
29. The Abbey Grange
30. The Reigate Squires
31. The Illustrious Client
32. The Three Gables
33. The Blanched Soldier
34. The Valley of Fear

35. A Study in Scarlet

36. Wisteria Lodge

37. The Retired Colourman

38. The Blanched Soldier

39. The Cardboard Box

40. The Sussex Vampire

41. A Study in Scarlet

42. The Hound of the Baskervilles

43. Wisteria Lodge

44. Thor Bridge

45. The Three Students

46. The Red Circle

47. The Disappearance of Lady Frances Carfax

48. The Six Napoleons

49. The Naval Treaty

50. The Engineer's Thumb

51. The Priory School

52. The Reigate Squires

53. The Beryl Coronet

54. The Second Stain

55. A Study in Scarlet

56. The Gloria Scott

57. The Six Napoleons

58. The Priory School

59. The Illustrious Client

60. The Bruce-Partington Plans

61. The Red-headed League

62. The Reigate Squires

63. The Greek Interpreter

64. The Greek Interpreter

65. The Red Circle

66. The Second Stain

67. The Red Circle

68. The Boscombe Valley Mystery

69. The Norwood Builder

70. The Valley of Fear

71. The Three Students

72. The Lion's Mane

73. The Valley of Fear

74. Shoscombe Old Place

75. The Valley of Fear

76. The Greek Interpreter

77. The Mazarin Stone

78. The Valley of Fear

79. The Hound of the Baskervilles

80. The Noble Bachelor

81. The Yellow Face

82. The Lion's Mane

83. Black Peter

84. The Bruce-Partington Plans

85. The Norwood Builder

86. The Five Orange Pips

87. The Missing Three-quarter

88. The Blue Carbuncle

89. The Naval Treaty

90. The Gloria Scott

91. The Creeping Man

92. The Stockbroker's Clerk

93. A Study in Scarlet

94. The Three Students

95. The Red-headed League

96. The Devil's Foot

97. The Speckled Band

98. The Copper Beeches

99. The Blue Carbuncle

100. The Man with the Twisted Lip

101. The Six Napoleons

102. The Hound of the Baskervilles

103. The Disappearance of Lady Frances Carfax

104. The Sign of Four

105. Silver Blaze

106. The Dancing Men

107. The Sign of Four

108. The Dying Detective

109. A Study in Scarlet

110. The Golden Pince-Nez

111. The Three Students

112. The Lion's Mane

113. A Study in Scarlet

114. The Hound of the Baskervilles

115. The Engineer's Thumb

116. The Missing Three-Quarter

117. The Final Problem

118. The Devil's Foot

119. The Three Gables

120. Silver Blaze

121. The Sign of Four

122. The Resident Patient

123. The Gloria Scott

124. The Boscombe Valley Mystery

125. His Last Bow

126. The Bruce-Partington Plans

127. The Bruce-Partington Plans

128. The Man with the Twisted Lip

129. The Priory School

130. The Solitary Cyclist

131. The Red-headed League

132. A Case of Identity

133. The Blue Carbuncle

134. The Crooked Man

135. The Solitary Cyclist

Which Case?

Answers

1. The Gloria Scott

2. His Last Bow

3. The Blanched Soldier

4. The Lion's Mane

5. A Scandal in Bohemia

6. The Five Orange Pips

7. A Study in Scarlet (December 1887)

8. Shoscombe Old Place (April 1927)

9. The Five Orange Pips

10. Wisteria Lodge

11. Thor Bridge

12. The Norwood Builder

13. The Three Gables

14. Lady Frances Carfax

15. The Engineer's Thumb

16. The Blanched Soldier

17. Abbey Grange

18. The Devil's Foot

19. The Veiled Lodger

20. The Boscombe Valley Mystery

21. The Five Orange Pips

22. The Resident Patient

23. The Musgrave Ritual

24. The Mazarin Stone

25. The Six Napoleons

26. The Beryl Coronet

27. The Blue Carbuncle

28. The Naval Treaty

29. Abbey Grange

30. The Hound of the Baskervilles

31. None, not in that precise way

32. The Speckled Band

33. The Retired Colourman

34. The Three Garridebs

35. The Illustrious Client

36. The Empty House

37. A Study in Scarlet

38. A Case of Identity

39. The Illustrious Client

40. The Mazarin Stone

41. The Musgrave Ritual

42. Shoscombe Old Place

43. The Dancing Men

44. Wisteria Lodge

45. The Reigate Squires

46. The Devil's Foot

47. The Dancing Men

48. The Solitary Cyclist

49. The Disappearance of Lady Frances Carfax

50. The Blue Carbuncle

Name the Character

Answers

1. Irene Adler
2. Ames
3. Dr. Leslie Armstrong
4. Henry Baker
5. James Barclay
6. Barker
7. Trevor Bennett
8. Beppo
9. Hugh Boone
10. James Browner
11. Hatty Doran
12. John Scott Eccles
13. Rev. J. C. Elman
14. Colonel Emsworth
15. John Ferrier
16. J. Neil Gibson
17. Inspector Gregory
18. Baron Adelbert Gruner
19. Annie Harrison
20. Henderson
21. Morse Hudson
22. Violet Hunter
23. Athelney Jones
24. Isadora Klein
25. Miles McLaren
26. John Mason
27. Melas
28. Colonel Sebastian Moran
29. Professor James Moriarty
30. Reginald Musgrave
31. Professor Presbury
32. Edith Presbury
33. Hall Pycroft
34. Daulat Ras

35. Rev. Roundhay

36. Ettie Shafter

37. Rev. Dr. Shlessinger

38. Abe Slaney

39. Willoughby Smith

40. Colonel Lysander Stark

41. Dr. Leon Sterndale

42. Mary Sutherland

43. Brenda Tregennis

44. James Trevor

45. Victor Trevor

46. von Bork

47. Jabez Wilson

48. Windigate

49. Kitty Winter

50. Theresa Wright

Scene of Action I, II, III

Answers

1.	Queene Anne Street	19.	Baron Gruner
2.	Irene Adler	20.	Stapleton
3.	Northumberland	21.	Irene Adler
4.	Jonas Oldacre	22.	*The Golden Pince-Nez*
5.	Louis La Rothiere	23.	*The Six Napoleons*
6.	Odessa	24.	St. James' Street
7.	Alexander Holder	25.	Rue De Trajan
8.	C	26.	Russell Square
9.	F	27.	St. Ives
10.	H	28.	San Francisco
11.	G	29.	Donnithorpe
12.	A	30.	St. Savior's, near King's Cross
13.	I	31.	St. George's, Hanover Square
14.	D	32.	Church of St. Monica on Edgware Road
15.	J	33.	Wisteria Lodge
16.	E	34.	The Andaman Islands
17.	B		
18.	Major John Sholto		

35. Mr. Melville
36. Hugo Oberstein
37. King's Cross
38. Carstairs in Kent
39. Charles
40. Charing Cross
41. Mr. Frankland
42. Langham
43. "Sally Dennis"
44. Diogenes
45. Cafe Royal
46. Norway
47. Florida
48. France
49. Nathan Garrideb
50. Francis Hay Moulton
51. Goodge Street
52. Swindon
53. Mr. and Mrs. Warren
54. Isadora Klein

55. Cecil James Barker
56. Dr. Hill Barton
57. Halifax, Nova Scotia
58. Hall Pycroft
59. Hampstead Heath
60. Lord Harringby
61. Horace Harker
62. Blackheath
63. Sherman
64. New Jersey
65. New Zealand
66. Abbas Parva
67. Adelarde, Australia
68. Algeria
69. Amoy in China
70. Belgrade
71. Brazil
72. Chicago
73. Cleveland
74. Atlanta

75. London

76. F and J

77. L

78. L

79. K

80. G

81. A

82. B

83. D

84. E

85. C

86. K

87. H

88. K

89. J

90. I

91. I

92. B

93. E

94. G

95. K

96. K

97. L

98. L

99. The Adairs

100. Outside the Holborn Bar

101. A chemistry laboratory at St. Bartholomew's Hospital

102. John Hector McFarlane

103. Bar of Gold in Upper Swandam Lane

104. Yorkshire

105. The British Museum

106. The Bagatelle

107. Barclay Square

108. General de Merville

109. Montague Street

110. Coburg Square

111. Colonel Sebastian Moran

112. Crane Water

113. Crewe

114. Crystal Palace

115. Dr. Horsum

116. Essex

117. Euston

118. James Baker Williams

119. Mauritius

120. Adolph Meyer

121. Grimpen

122. Watt Street Chapel, Aldershot

123. Don Juan Murillo

124. Holder and Stevenson

125. Hurlingham

126. Inner Temple

127. Latimer's

128. Enoch Drebber

129. John Scott Eccles

130. Capital and Countries Bank at the Oxford Street branch

131. Minories

132. Count Sylvius

133. Netley

134. Norbury

135. Oxford

136. Pernambuco, Brazil

137. Poldhu Bay

138. Duncan Ross

139. Portsdown Hill

140. Portsmouth

141. Rome

142. Henri Fournaye and his wife

143. Stives

144. St. James' Hall

145. Silvester's Bank

146. Lord Southerton

147. Sussex

148. Dr. Leon Sterndale

149. Little Purlington

150. A mental hospital — where Amberley was presumably heading

Matching Sets

Answers

1. (a)	10. (a)	18. (c)
2. (b)	11. (b)	19. (a)
3. (c)	12. (b)	20. (e)
4. (d)	13. (a)	21. (d)
5. (e)	14. (b)	22. (e)
6. (c)	15. (c)	23. (a)
7. (d)	16. (b)	24. (b)
8. (e)	17. (e)	25. (a)
9. (a)		

Holmes and His Disguises

Answers

1. C	6. J	11. H
2. D	7. I	12. B
3. E	8. K	13. A
4. F	9. L	14. D
5. G	10. H	

The Animal Kingdom

Answers

1. The Sign of Four
2. The Copper Beeches
3. Silver Blaze
4. The Missing Three-Quarter
5. The Hound of the Baskervilles
6. The Sussex Vampire
7. The Creeping Man
8. The Lion's Mane
9. Shoscombe Old Place
10. The "Gloria Scott"
11. The Lion's Mane
12. Sahara King
13. A giant sea medusa, Cyanea Capillata
14. A horse
15. A snake
16. Iris
17. A crocodile in the Ganges River
18. Jeremy Dixon
19. Colonel Ross
20. Teddy

Inns and Hotels

Answers

1. C
2. G
3. H
4. D
5. I
6. A
7. A
8. B
9. E
10. F

On the High Seas

Answers

1. F

2. C, M

3. I

4. B

5. O, A, E, H

6. N

7. D

8. L

9. K

10. J

11. G

Genius at Work

Answers

1. Feeble

2. Variable

3. Nil

4. Accurate but unsystematic

5. Nil

6. Profound

7. Nil

8. Practical but limited

9. Immense

10. Violin

11. Swordsman

12. Law

13. Thoreau

14. Balzac

15. The brothers Grimm

16. George Meredith

17. *The Crooked Man*

18. Goethe

19. Winwood Reade's *Martyrdom of Man*

20. *Practical Handbook of Bee Culture with Some Observations upon the Segregation of the Queen*

21. *Upon the Polyphonic Motets of Lassus*

22. *The Whole Art of Detection*

23. The Bible

24. Whitakers

25. Hafiz

26. Petrarch

27. Chaldean

28-30. Miracle plays
Medieval pottery
Stradivarius violins
The Buddhism of Ceylon
The warships of the future

Unpublished Cases

Answers

1.	Aluminum	19.	Savage
2.	Camberwell	20.	Bishopgate
3.	Tosca	21.	French
4.	Coptic	22.	Parva
5.	Leech	23.	Upwood
6.	Rat	24.	Captain
7.	Trepoff	25.	Laundry
8.	Paradol	26.	Locking-up
9.	Cormorant	27.	Madness
10.	Ricoletti	28.	Forger
11.	Yeggman	29.	Poisoner
12.	Baltimore	30.	Canary-Trainer
13.	Vamberry	31.	Venomous
14.	Russian	32.	Wonder
15.	Darlington	33.	Belle
16.	Mendicant	34.	Terror
17.	Murderer	35.	Turkey
18.	Dundas		

Words of Wisdom I & II

Answers

1. religion	19. gregarious
2. horrible	20. commonplace
3. detection	21. soul
4. Providence	22. forgiveness
5. improbable	23. Fate
6. method	24. compensation
7. data	25. jest
8. vital	26. suffering
9. bizarre	27. impatient
10. examined	28. futile
11. cocaine bottle	29. little
12. criminal	30. imagination
13. agony	31. ghosts
14. rusty	32. Nature
15. racing engine	33. overlook
16. fixed scale	34. typewriter
17. silence	35. Singularity
18. companion	36. Circumstantial

37.	alias	57.	unravel
38.	deficiencies	58.	inch
39.	common	59.	tracing
40.	logic	60.	footsteps
41.	countryside	61.	everything
42.	age	62.	sweep
43.	contagious	63.	Moriarty
44.	discover	64.	inscrutable
45.	change	65.	insoluble
46.	secretive	66.	drifting
47.	alternative	67.	trusted
48.	first	68.	bias
49.	revenge	69.	consequence
50.	difficulty	70.	Pipes
51.	complex	71.	press
52.	thought	72.	family
53.	intersection	73.	Dogs
54.	exceptions	74.	Toby
55.	scarlet	75.	music
56.	colourless	76.	portraits

77. reincarnation

78. *Times*

79. educated

80. violin

81. Misdeeds

82. Professor Moriarty

83. Archives

84. commonplace

85. details

86. science

87. evidence

88. Circumstantial

89. Education

90. emotional

91. first

92. scheming

93. starve

94. stimulating

95. changing

96. blank

97. attic

98. furniture

99. immortal

100. sorrow

101. unnatural

102. wicked

103. purposeless

104. courage

105. rash

106. devil

107. conjurer

108. details

109. test

110. emotions

111. rose

112. discover

113. testimonials

114. observes

115. imagination

116. science

117. hiding

118. Slips

119. facts

120. violence

121. opportunities

122. realistic

123. discreet

124. nettle

125. rule

126. convincing

127. decently

128. special

129. trumps

130. honest

131. direct

132. attack

133. eagles

134. strike

135. trifles

136. fact

137. prejudices

138. reasoner

139. future

140. events

141. Familiarity

142. err

143. strange

144. insufficient

145. Marengo

146. knowledge

147. odd

148. prove

149. interplay

150. extraordinary

Sir Arthur Conan Doyle

Answers

1. 1859

2. Edinburgh

3. Member of Parliament

4. Roman Catholic

5. Spiritualism

6. Stonyhurst College

7. Southsea

8. 1902

9. No. 2 Devonshire Place, London

10. Jean Leckie (his second wife)

11. The Belgian Congo in his *The Crime of the Congo*

12. Oscar Slater

13. Louise Hawkins (nick-named Touie)

14. f

15. b

16. g

17. a

18. c

19. d

20. e

The Scions

Answers

1. C

2. H

3. K

4. A

5. J

6. B

7. L

8. D

9. E

10. F

11. G

12. I

13. M

14. T

15. S

16. N

17. Q

18. O

19. P

20. R

Miscellany I

Answers

1. Mycroft Holmes

2. It is the study of snakes

3. Dr. Shlessinger

4 . Jefferson Hope

5. Documents, especially those connected with his past cases (*The Musgrave Ritual*)

6. About half

7. The Latin countries

8. *The Retired Colourman*

9. Crockford

10. Mr. Barker

11. Josiah Amberley

12. The Turkish bath (*The Illustrious Client*)

13. Shinwell Johnson

14. Anthony Boucher

15. The French painter Vernet

16. The Valley of Fear

17. Opera singer (a contralto)

18. The Man who was Wanted

19. Orchid

20. Dr. Joseph Bell

21. *Beeton's Christmas Annual*

22. *Lippincott's*

23. *The Strand*

24. Sidney Paget

25. The Baker Street Irregulars

26. Mrs. Hudson

27. 1934

28. Franklin D. Roosevelt

29. Harry Truman

30. Christ Cella's

31. *The Blue Carbuncle*

32. Yellow-back novels

33. Afghan

34. Dr. Thorneycroft Huxtable in *The Priory School*

35. Northumberland Street, just off Trafalgar Square

36. The Great Hiatus — so dubbed by A. Carson Simpson

37. 1854 because Holmes is referred to as "tall, gaunt and 60 years old" in *His Last Bow*, which occurred in 1914

38. Bradley's

39. The new schools of Britain

40. Sanger

41. J

42. D

43. A

44. B

45. F

46. D

47. I

48. E

49. H

50. G

Miscellany II

Answers

1. Professor Coram

2. Cox and Co.

3. Shinwell Johnson (*The Illustrious Client*)

4. Flowers (in *The Naval Treaty*)

5. Grace Dunbar

6. Mrs. Gibson

7. Jimmy Griggs

8. Colonel Sebastian Moran

9. Roman Catholic

10. Corot

11. Watson in *The Naval Treaty*

12. Victor Trevor

13. Sir Eustace Brackenstall

14. Dr. Moore Agar

15. Sir Jasper Meek

16. Dr. Ainstree

17. Alexis

18. Josiah Barnes

19. Marlow Bates

20. Holmes. It was a magazine article on the science of deduction

21. In a Persian slipper

22. Sir John Gielgud

23. Sir Ralph Richardson

24. Orson Welles

25. Brandy

26. Calcutta

27. Cardinal Tosca

28. Central Press Syndicate

29. Chinese Pottery

30. Chopin

31. Sir Colin

32. Prince of Colonna

33. The Daily Telegraph

34-36. Mahomet Singh, Dost Akbar, Abdullah Khan, and Jonathan Small

37. Earl of Dovercourt

38. Professor Moriarty

39. J. C. Elman

40. Farquhar

41. Captain Ferguson

42. A Creole

43. Baron Adelbert Gruner

44. Reuben Hayes

45. Lord Holdhurst

46. John Horner

47. Mrs. Turner

48. Huguenot

49. Hyams

50. Dr. Jackson

51. Sidney Johnson

52. Legion of Honour

53. Leonardo

54. Lomax, the sub-librarian of London Library

55. Maudsley

Miscellany III

Answers

1. Countess of Morcar

2-3. Cocaine and morphine

4. Bevington

5. Charlie Peace

6. James Phillimore

7. Maria Pinto

8. Bartholomew Sholto (also a police inspector)

9. Rodger Prescott

10. Francis Prosper

11. Mr. Roundhay

12. Lord Saltine

13. Dr. Thorneycroft Huxtable

14. Elias Whitney

15. Dr. Grimesby Roylott

16. Aldwych

17. Toronto

18. 1951

19. John Murray

20. Sidney Paget of London

21. Frederic Doar Steele of New York

22. A jack-knife

23. "Killer Evans"

24. Holmes' article *The Book of Life*

25. Queen Victoria

26. *The Exploits of Sherlock Holmes*

27. John Clay, the mysterious assistant in *The Red-Headed League*

28. Battle of Maiwand (July 7, 1880)

29. Peshawar

30. "Enteric fever"

31. Jezail

32. The Literary Agent

33. Cocaine

34. Three times a day

35. Hosmer Angel

36. The King of Bohemia

37. Hamish (in her *Unpopular Opinions* p. 148)

38. Henry Baker

39. Dr. Grimesby Roylott

40. "A customs official who boards incoming ships to check the observance of customs regulations" (Dakin, p. 87)

41. Violet Hunter

42. Violet Smith

43. Violet Westbury

44. Violet de Merville

45. Dr. Anstruther

46. "A blazing hot day in August"

47. Wilson Kemp

48. "Bude-Pesth" (Budapest)

49. Von Herder

50. Dr. Shlessinger, alias Holy Peters

51. Mycroft

52. Amberley

53. *The Three Gables*

The Higher Criticism

Answers

1. Mollie and Michael Hardwick

2. Gavin Brend

3. Trevor Hall

4. Michael Harrison

5. Vincent Starrett

6. William Baring-Gould

7. Sir Sydney Roberts

8. Martin Dakin

9. Michael Harrison

10. William Baring-Gould

11. James Edward Holroyd

12. T. S. Blakeney

13. Jay Finley Christ

14. Rex Stout

15. Ronald Knox in his *Essays in Satire*

16. Heywood Broun

17. Howard Collins

18. Dorothy L. Sayers

19. Ellery Queen

20. Christopher Morley

21. Guy Warrack

22. Vincent Starrett

23. Monsignor Ronald Knox

24. Edward van Liere

25. Edgar Smith

26-29. *The Blanched Soldier*
The Lion's Mane
The Mazarin Stone
The Three Gables
(see Dakin's *A Sherlock Holmes Commentary* pp. 249-252)

30. Trevor Hall in his *The Late Mr. Sherlock Holmes*

31. e

32. d

33. c

34. b

35. a

The Distaff Side

Answers

1. A Scandal in Bohemia
2. The Golden Pince-Nez
3. The Lion's Mane
4. The Abbey Grange
5. Wisteria Lodge
6. The Dancing Men
7. The Cardboard Box
8. The Disappearance of Lady Frances Carfax
9. The Sussex Vampire
10. The Noble Bachelor
11. Thor Bridge
12. The Musgrave Ritual
13. The Copper Beeches
14. The Three Gables
15. The Hound of the Baskervilles
16. The Three Gables
17. The Illustrious Client
18. The Noble Bachelor
19. The Sign of Four
20. The Beryl Coronet
21. The Veiled Lodger
22. The Valley of Fear
23. The Solitary Cyclist
24. The Speckled Band
25. A Case of Identity
26. The Devil's Foot
27. The Red Circle
28. The Bruce-Partington Plans
29. The Illustrious Client
30. The Abbey Grange

The Constabulary

Answers

1. b	10. a	19. Tobias Gregson
2. c	11. f	20. Aberdonian
3. c	12. g	21. Inspector Baynes
4. c	13. g	22. The Reigate Puzzle
5. d	14. f	23. Lestrade
6. e	15. g	24. The Sign of Four
7. a (also Baynes)	16. f	25. Lestrade
8. c	17. f	
9. c	18. c	

All Numbers

Answers

1. 3

2. 4

3. 6

4. 3

5. 5

6. 3

7. 56

8. 4

9. 17

10. 55 shillings

11. 17 (though almost all chronologists believe the actual figure to be much higher)

12. at least 2, Colonel Moriarty and a younger brother who was a station master in the west of England

13. £6,000

14. XX31

15. £25

16. 7

17. 140 (Sign of Four)

18. 42 (Priory School)

19. 75 (The Hound of the Baskervilles)

20. 5 (Black Peter)

Nicknames and Aliases

Answers

1. Ted Baldwin
2. Captain Peter Carey
3. Shinwell Johnson
4. John Turner
5. Hugo Oberstein
6. Jonas Oldacre
7. John Clay
8. Colonel Lysander Stark
9. John Straker
10. Sherlock Holmes
11. Dr. Shlessinger
12. John Garrideb
13. Sherlock Holmes
14. John Ryder
15. Don Juan Murillo
16. Charles Augustus Milverton
17. Colonel Sebastian Moran
18. Professor Moriarty
19. Fred Porlock
20. John McGinty

Born to the Purple

Answers

1. Sir
2. Lord
3. Lord
4. Baron
5. Duke
6. Lord
7. Lord
8. Sir
9. Lord
10. Lord
11. Count
12. Baron
13. Sir
14. Sir
15. Sir

Sherlockian Scramble

Answers

1.	Leonardo	18.	Ronder
2.	Gorgiano	19.	Sterndale
3.	Gilchrist	20.	Reigate
4.	Kensington	21.	Wisteria
5.	Saunders	22.	von Bork
6.	Southerton	23.	Shlessinger
7.	Stapleton	24.	Sholto
8.	Gennaro Lucca	25.	Hookah
9.	Lowenstein	26.	Drebber
10.	Nana Sahib	27.	Huxtable
11.	Musgrave	28.	Godfrey Norton
12.	Pierrot	29.	Black Swan
13.	Baron Cuvier	30.	Isadora Klein
14.	Dartmoor	31.	Kirwan
15.	Hatherley	32.	Paul Kratides
16.	Gruner	33.	Mycroft
17.	Milverton	34.	Watson

35.	Marker	55.	Brambletye Hotel
36.	Marylebone	56.	Lestrade
37.	Maudsley	57.	Leicester
38.	Merrilow	58.	Jonas Oldacre
39.	Pinchin Lane	59.	Victor Lynch
40.	Pinner	60.	Laura Lyons
41.	Thurston	61.	Mary Morstan
42.	Garrideb	62.	Naval Treaty
43.	Victor Trevor	63.	Sussex Vampire
44.	Westaway	64.	Selden
45.	Westville Arms	65.	Leslie Oakshott
46.	Williamson	66.	Odessa
47.	Maiwand	67.	Peshawur
48.	Bombay	68.	Persano
49.	Bloomsbury	69.	Persian Slipper
50.	Blackheath	70.	Hudson
51.	Charing Cross	71.	Petersfield
52.	Tibet	72.	Pompey
53.	Hafiz	73.	Diogenes Club
54.	Illustrious Client	74.	Susan Dobney

75. Ian Murdoch

76. Carlo

77. Cunningham

78. James Mortimer

79. Moriarty

80. Edgware Road

81. Birdy Edwards

82. Edmonton Street

83. Killer Evans

84. Esmeralda

85. Englischer Hof

86. Euston Station

87. Emsworth

88. Retired Colourman

89. Blue Carbuncle

90. Abdullah Khan

91. Saxe-Coburg Square

92. Lowenstein

93. Maberley

94. Mazarin Stone

95. Reichenbach Falls

96. Ricoletti

97. Jephro Rucastle

98. Mahomet Singh

99. Simpson

100. Sigerson

Colours

Answers

1.	Red	12.	Red
2.	Scarlet	13.	Red
3.	Blue	14.	Brown
4.	Yellow	15.	Green
5.	Orange	16.	Brown
6.	Red	17.	Green
7.	Silver	18.	Black
8.	Black	19.	Gray
9-11.	blue, purple, mouse	20.	Black

The Hired Help

Answers

1. Billy

2. Wiggins

3. Mercer

4. Ames

5. Edith Baxter

6. Dolores

7. Willoughby Smith

8. William Kirwan

9. MacPhail

10. Mary Jane

11. Michael

12. John Mitton

13. Mortimer

14. Old Ralph

15. John Barrymore

16. Stephens

17. Westaways

18. Susan Tarlton

19. Theresa Wright

20. Carrie Evans Norlett

On Stage and Screen

Answers

1. Eille Norwood

2. Sadler's Wells

3. Raymond Massey

4. Clive Brook

5. Basil Rathbone

6. Peter Cushing

7. Carleton Hobbs

8. The Private Lives of Sherlock Holmes

9. Robert Stephens

10. Billy Wilder

11. Baker Street

12. Fritz Weaver

13. John Barrymore (surprise!)

14. Charlie Chaplin (another surprise!)

15. Arthur Wontner

16. William Gillette

17. Nigel Bruce

18-19. *A Study in Scarlet, The Return of Sherlock Holmes*

20. Reginald Owen

Food and Drink

Answers

1. The Dying Detective

2. Tokay — "Another glass, Watson"

3. Simpsons

4. Claret

5. Thor Bridge

6. Two hard boiled eggs

7. Oysters and grouse

8. The Naval Treaty

9. Mr. and Mrs. Francis Hay Moulton

10. Breakfast

11. Green peas

Colonels

Answers

1. F

2. J

3. A

4. I

5. B

6. H

7. E

8. D

9. G

10. C

Scoring

	Number of Questions	Number Right			
		Superlative	Capital	Elementary	Back to the Canon!
Which Case I	50	45-50	35-44	25-34	0-24
Miscellany I, II, III	50, 55, 53	45-	35-44	25-34	0-24
Scene of Action I, II, III	50, 50, 50	45-50	35-44	25-34	0-24
Unpublished Cases	35	32-35	24-31	18-23	0-17
Food and Drink	11	10-11	8-9	6-7	0-5
Words of Wisdom I	100	90-100	70-89	50-69	0-49
Words of Wisdom II	50	45-50	35-44	25-34	0-24
Nicknames and Aliases	20	18-20	14-17	10-13	0-9
All Numbers	20	18-20	14-17	10-13	0-9
The Constabulary	25	23-25	18-22	13-17	0-12
On Stage and Screen	20	18-20	14-17	10-13	0-9
Born to the Purple	15	13-15	10-14	8-9	0-7
The Hired Help	20	18-20	14-17	10-13	0-9
Who's Who I, II, III	50, 50, 35*	45-50	35-44	25-34	0-24
The Distaff Side	30	27-30	21-26	15-20	0-14
The Higher Criticism	35	32-35	24-31	18-23	0-17
Genius at Work	30	27-30	21-26	15-20	0-14
Name the Character	50	45-50	35-44	25-34	0-24
The Animal Kingdom	20	18-20	14-17	10-13	0-9
On the High Seas	15	13-15	10-14	8-9	0-7
Inns and Hotels	10	9-10	7-8	5-6	0-4
Disguises	14	13-14	10-12	7-9	0-6
Matching Sets	25	23-25	18-22	13-17	0-12
Colours	20	18-20	14-17	10-13	0-9
Sir Arthur Conan Doyle	20	18-20	14-17	10-13	0-9
The Scions	20	18-20	14-17	10-13	0-9
Colonels	10	9-10	7-8	5-6	0-4

* Same as others with 35.

A Selective Directory of the Societies

The Arkansas Valley Investors, Ltd.
Jason Rouby
P. O. Box 2233
Little Rock, Ark. 72203

The Baker Street Irregulars
Dr. Julian Wolff
33 Riverside Drive
New York, N.Y. 10023

The Bootmakers of Toronto
Cameron Hollyer
Metropolitan Toronto Central Library
214 College St.
Toronto 2B, Ontario, Canada

The Brothers Three of Moriarty
John Bennett Shaw
1917 Fort Union Dr.
Santa Fe, N.M. 87501

The Confederates of Wisteria Lodge
Robert S. Gellerstedt, Jr.
2551 Meadow Lark Dr.
East Point, Ga. 30344

The Council of Four
Robert C. Peterson
2845 S. Gilpen St.
Denver, Colo. 80210

The Creeping Men of Cleveland
William McCullam
Fairmont Rd.
Newbury, Ohio 44065

The Crew of the Barque *Lone Star*
Margaret F. Morris
472 Westview Terrace
Arlington, Texas 76013

The Cornish Horrors
Rev. Henry T. Folsom
338 Main St.
Old Saybrook, Conn. 06475

The Five Orange Pips of
Westchester County, N.Y.
Richard W. Clarke
Holly Branch Rd.
Katonah, N.Y.

The Greek Interpreters
Donald A. Yates
537 Wells Hall
Michigan State University
East Lansing, Mich. 48823

The Hounds of the Baskerville (sic)
Robert W. Hahn
509 S. Ahrens
Lombard, Ill. 60148

The Hudson Valley Sciontists
Glenn V. Laxton
Orchard Rd.
Poughkeepsie, N.Y. 12603

Hugo's Companions
Robert W. Hahn
509 S. Ahrens
Lombard, Ill. 60148

The Maiwand Jezails
Richard D. Lesh
505 E. 10th St.
Wayne, Neb. 68787

The Masters Class
Robert M. Broderick
Township Linerd
Ewynedd Valley, Pa. 19437

The Noble Bachelors (and
Concubines) of St. Louis
Philip A. Shreffler
827 W. Rose Hill
Kirkwood, Mo. 63122

The Non-Canonical Calabashes of
Los Angeles
John Farrell
1367 W. 6th St.
San Pedro, Calif. 90732

The Norwegian Explorers
E. W. McDiarmid
1473 Fulham St.
St. Paul, Minn. 55108

The Old Soldiers of Baker Street
W. T. (Bill) Rabe
909 Prospect
Sault Sainte Marie, Mich. 49783

The Old Soldiers of Praed Street
Theodore G. Schulz
180 Mt. Lassen Dr.
San Rafael, Calif. 94903

The Pleasant Places of Florida
Leslie Marshall
P. O. Box 386
St. Petersburg, Fla. 33731

The Praed Street Irregulars
Luther Norris
3844 Watseka Ave.
Culver City, Calif. 90230

The Priory Scholars
Chris Steinbrunner
62-52 82nd St.
Middle Village, N.Y. 11379

The Red Circle
Peter E. Blau
4107 W. St., NW, Apt. 200
Washington, D.C. 20007

The Resident Patients of Baker Street
Valerie Hill
6760 South West 76th Terrace
South Miami, Fla. 33143

The Scandalous Bohemians of
New Jersey
Norman S. Nolan
68 Crest Rd.
Middleton, N.J. 07748

The Scion of the Four
Andrew G. Fusco
643 Trovato Dr.
Morgantown, W.Va. 26505

The Scowrers and Molly Maguires
Dean Dickensheet
2430 Lake St., Apt. 7
San Francisco, Calif. 94121

Sherlock Holmes Klubben i Danmark
(The Danish Baker Street Irregulars)
Henry Lauritzen
Tegner, Vesterbro 60
9000 Aalborg, Denmark

The Sherlock Holmes Society of London
Lord Donegall
The Studio
39 Clabon Mews
London, S.W. 1, England

The Six Napoleons of Baltimore
Steve Clarkson
3612 Briarstone Rd.
Randallstown, Md. 21133

The Solitary Cyclists of Sweden
Ted Bergman
Storkvägen 10
181 35 Lidingö, Sweden

The Sons of the Copper Beeches
John B. Koelle
244 Haverford Ave.
Swarthmore, Pa. 19081

The Speckled Band
James Keddie, Jr.
28 Laurel Ave.
Wellesley Hills, Mass. 02181

The Sub-Librarians Scion of
B.S.I. in A.L.A.
Margaret F. Morris
472 Westview Terrace
Arlington, Texas 76013

The Sub-Librarians Scion of the
Sherlock Holmes Society of London
within the Canadian Library
Association
David Skene Melvin
36 Chapel St.
Brampton, Ontario, Canada

The Trifling Monographs
Lucy Chase Williams
1783 Yale Station
New Haven, Conn. 06520

The William Gilliam Gillette
Memorial Luncheon
Lisa McGaw
392 Central Park West
New York, N.Y. 10025